Job
Interview

Amaze the Interviewer With Your Body Language
and Get Your Dream Job Fast

(The Topic and Answer and Faqs You Need to
Know to Get the Job)

Misha Yate

Published by Rob Miles

Misha Yate

All Rights Reserved

Job Interview: Amaze the Interviewer With Your Body Language and Get Your Dream Job Fast (The Topic and Answer and Faqs You Need to Know to Get the Job)

ISBN 978-1-989990-63-6

All rights reserved. No part of this guide may be reproduced in any form without permission in writing from the publisher except in the case of brief quotations embodied in critical articles or reviews.

Legal & Disclaimer

The information contained in this book is not designed to replace or take the place of any form of medicine or professional medical advice. The information in this book has been provided for educational and entertainment purposes only.

The information contained in this book has been compiled from sources deemed reliable, and it is accurate to the best of the Author's knowledge; however, the Author cannot guarantee its accuracy and validity and cannot be held liable for any errors or omissions. Changes are periodically made to this book. You must consult your doctor or get professional medical advice before using any of the suggested remedies, techniques, or information in this book.

Upon using the information contained in this book, you agree to hold harmless the Author from and against any damages, costs, and expenses, including any legal fees potentially resulting from the application of any of the information provided by this guide. This disclaimer applies to any damages or injury caused by the use and application, whether directly or indirectly, of any advice or information presented, whether for breach of contract, tort, negligence, personal injury, criminal intent, or under any other cause of action.

You agree to accept all risks of using the information presented inside this book. You need to consult a professional medical practitioner in order to ensure you are both able and healthy enough to participate in this program.

Table of Contents

INTRODUCTION 1

CHAPTER 1: PREPARATIONS 3

CHAPTER 2: ASSESSING YOURSELF 20

CHAPTER 3: HOW TO PREPARE YOURSELF FOR A JOB INTERVIEW? 24

CHAPTER 4: USE TECHNOLOGY WISELY 36

CHAPTER 5: THE BASICS OF SALES 41

CHAPTER 6: "FIRST IMPRESSIONS" 44

CHAPTER 7: HOW TO STAND OUT IN TODAY'S COMPETITIVE MARKET 57

CHAPTER 8: CLOSING QUESTIONS 67

CHAPTER 9: SITUATIONAL INTERVIEW QUESTIONS 75

CHAPTER 10: TOP JOB INTERVIEW QUESTIONS 79

CHAPTER 11: HOW TO SEARCH FOR AN INTERVIEW OPPORTUNITY 97

CHAPTER 12: THE INTERVIEW 108

CHAPTER 13: GROUNDWORK FOR INTERVIEW 113

CHAPTER 14: WHAT IS THE SECRET TO LANDING THAT NEW JOB 123

CHAPTER 15: BODY LANGUAGE: TIPS FOR A CONFIDENT AND POSITIVE BODY LANGUAGE 127

CHAPTER 16: WHAT TO PREPARE BEFORE AN INTERVIEW 135

CHAPTER 17: YOUR FOCUS.. 142

CHAPTER 18: CRAFTING YOUR COVER LETTER............... 157

CONCLUSION.. 178

Introduction

You've had your dream job in the back of your mind for years. Perhaps you have been working in other fields but you have never been able to quite shake the idea of working in the position you have always wanted. Maybe you have been passed up for job promotions time and time again despite having the proper qualifications and you are asking yourself what you can do differently. Much of the time the difference between you landing the job you want and deserve comes down to your interview!

It seems like a silly thing, the difference between your dreams coming true or continuing to work in positions which keep those dreams at an arms length is your interview, but it is true! Within the pages of this book we will discuss the secrets to landing your job through interview techniques which will set you apart from the other candidates, boost your confidence, and answer questions which will help give you an edge over the other candidates. The time to land the position of your dreams is now!

Chapter 1: Preparations

Every journey to success starts with extensive preparation. You cannot run a marathon or bake a cake successfully without an ample amount of preparation. The first impressions that you make during the interview need to be perfected behind the screens first. There is nothing worse than a candidate showing up for an interview with incomplete documents and no knowledge of the responsibilities of the job they are applying for. Even the most confident of people can get nervous at the sound of an interview. And rightfully so! Recruiters are not just looking at your qualifications but even the little personality traits that probably even you didn't know exist. However, all those nerves and jitters can be calmed down by simply preparing. Preparations take the guesswork out of the interview. By understanding what the recruiters expect of you and preparing for

it, you take control of the situation by a large extent.
Following are a list of things you need to prepare for in advance:

Get Your Documents in Order

You have already submitted your resume to the company; they have already gone through it and would probably have it on them when they call you for the interview, right?

How about the interviewer goes, 'Hey mate, I don't have a copy of your resume with me, do you have one on you right now?' Well, you could tell him you already sent one in and that is why we're called for the interview, or you could simply just take one out and hand it to him. Better still, take three out, one for each of the interviewers. How awesome would that be? You should have all the important documents with you when you for the interview, regardless of whether or not you have already sent them in. Following is a list of the important documents you should have on you:

v Copies of Your Resume: **It is** recommended to keep five copies with you. Not only to hand them out to all the interviewers, but what if the company is in a rush to hire? You do well through the first round, and the hiring manager schedules another interview with the department head or the boss right after? You'd want some extra copies on you just in case. It is always better to have more copies than you expect you'll need.

v **Your Reference List:** This is usually asked after the first round of interviews. But it is always better to be prepared. Businesses usually ask around your previous workplace and/or customers to get a better understanding of your skills and work ethics.

v **Recommendation Letters:** Recommendation letters are a great little souvenir to leave behind for the hiring manager to look at post-interview. Do not bring the original recommendation letters with you. You should always make copies and leave the original at home. Say you have three recommendations, get copies, staple each set together and offer one set at the end of the interview.

v **Your Driver's License:** Your driver's license is usually required to serve as a picture identification document. You will most likely need this at the time of hiring, but it is advised to keep a copy with you at the time of the interview also.

v **Social Security Card:** In case you don't have a driver's license. You could use a copy of your social security card for the same purpose.

v **Passport:** This is again for the same purpose. It is not always necessary unless the position you are applying for requires a lot of overseas trips. Many companies also ask for two picture identification documents, so if you don't have a driver's license, then your passport can be used for the same.

v **Academic Certificates:** These include your proof of education and should include your degrees, diplomas, and any other accredited certifications.

v **Business Cards:** This might sound old-school, but it is a small piece of paper that is easy to store with all the important information to get in touch with you. Your interviewer would definitely give you extra points for it.

v **Portfolio of Work:** If you have a portfolio, then do bring it with you to let your work do most of the talking. Many people believe portfolios are limited to design and arts. But you can bring portfolios of projects like marketing promotions, advertisements, etc. Whatever work that you can present on paper, bring it with you. Your portfolio can really help set you apart from other candidates as it offers a demonstration of the quality of the work you can provide.

v **Fact Sheet:** This is more for you than it is for the hiring manager. This sheet should have all the information that could be required by HR. It should include proper names, telephone numbers, addresses, start and end dates at previous workplaces, links to LinkedIn, and other online work profiles. Most companies would request you to submit this paperwork. So rather than searching through all the documents and calling up your partner to ask for proper addresses, it would look more professional and make things easier for you to have everything handy on a single paper.

v **A Paper and Pen:** This is interview prep 101- ALWAYS HAVE A PAPER AND NOTEPAD WITH YOU! You don't want to be asking the hiring manager for this, or worse just nodding your head at all that they say without taking notes. It makes you look more interested if you take notes about job specifications or other important information. However, be sure to ask the interviewer if it is alright for you to take notes.

v **Talking Points:** There are so many things that you want to speak to your interviewer about. Maybe dump in that little information about the company that you had followed up on online. But with nerves and questions being fired at you, it could be difficult to remember all that information. When you have a list of things you want to speak to your interviewer about, you can remain calm and focused.

v **A List of Questions for the Interviewer:** We will discuss in more detail later in the book, but it makes sense to have the list of questions with you. It shows that you have prepared for the interview. Showing up for an interview with proper documents not only makes you look like a professional, but is also a sign of respect for everyone's time. You could tell the interviewer you'd 'e-mail the missing documents,' but you are in a way telling them that you don't have any regard for their time.

Make the Documents Pretty and Professional Looking

First impressions are all about professionalism, and you want to exuberate the same through not just the way you talk, walk and dress, but also how you present your documents. Following are a number of do's and don'ts to help you make your documents more professional looking:

v Keep all your documents in a clean and

crisp folder. You will be bringing a lot of paperwork with you, so it makes sense to have it all in a manageable folder. You don't rummage through a bag for a piece of crumpled paper as proof of your professionalism. This simple act will instantly make you look more organized.

v Do not staple your resume and cover letter together. Though both these would be presented at the same time, it makes more sense to have them untied. The interviewer wouldn't want to keep the cover letter for future references but probably would want to keep the resume handy.

v Do not fold the documents. You don't want them to have lines in case the interviewer would like to get copies. Also, flat sheets of paper look crisper and more presentable.

v It is better to get new copies rather than use old ones if they look worn out. Avoid holding them with oily or dirty hands, it may not seem obvious or significant, but when in the hands of a hiring manager scrutinizing everything, even a small coffee stain could make a huge negative impact. v Laminate any certificates and original documents.

Eco-Friendly Documents

More and more businesses are adopting greener and environment-friendly alternatives. Using recycled paper, or better still, offering soft copies could be extremely helpful. Especially if during your research, you find out the company you are applying to adopts greener alternatives, then it could offer a great opportunity to make a positive impact. Following are a few notes to keep in mind:

Be sure to request the same via e-mail. Ask if the recruiters would be comfortable with soft copies.

Construct the resume in the body of the e-mail rather than adding an attachment. Due to fear of viruses, many companies are not comfortable with opening attachments.
Don't be drinking coffee in paper cups and eating a hot dog off a disposable plate in

the waiting area. Someone might notice, and they wouldn't really buy into your claims of adopting a greener lifestyle.

Select the right words. Just because you have an eco-friendly approach does not give you the right to judge the business's practice. Be respectful and thoughtful and avoid giving off ideas for greener options for the company. You'd have plenty of time for that once hired.

Get Stellar References

References are an integral part of the job screening process. They allow your prospective employers to check if you really are worth an investment in their company. Checking up on references enables them to understand your work ethics, your skill levels, and your dedication to your job. Following are a number of factors to keep in mind when preparing your reference letter:

Preparing the Reference List

v References don't have to be limited to your previous bosses. You can offer references of customers, former colleagues, human resource, management and pretty much anyone else that can attest to your qualifications. Don't just limit references to your previous workplace, if you have volunteered somewhere, took up an internship or any other related paid work that you may have done can be used to list references.
v Under NO circumstances, list family and friends as references. You can, though use coaches and mentors.
v Do not select someone whom you have not directly worked with or cannot provide ample or correct information about your work.
v Do not use references of people who are not related to the industry that you are applying in.
v Always speak to the references and ask their permission before putting them down for the same. You would also want to confirm their position and contact details. They may not be working at the

same company anymore, or the contact information might be outdated. Nothing worse than having the recruiter call up a reference and find out the contact details are wrong. Also, ask them how they are most comfortable to be contacted- via phone or email.
v Don't list too many references. If you are confused between a number of people, opt for those whom you have worked for longer than six months and/or those who can provide information related to the duties of the job you are currently applying to.
v Describe your relationship with the person listed as a reference; this will help the interviewer to ask targeted and related questions. You may also want to add specific skills that the reference can vouch for.

Formatting

v Use the same fonts, style, and type of paper as you used for your resume. This makes it more professional looking and easier to identify.

v List your name and contact information on top of the page.
v Opt for a list format rather than paragraphs. This makes it easier for the recruiter to locate information.
v Separate each set of reference with two spaces making it visually appealing and easier to read through. So if the recruiter would like to speak to someone about your ability to manage teams, they can easily scour through the list and find the person most suitable to contact for that information.

Should You or Shouldn't You Offer References?

Now there is a bit of a debate over this. Many hiring managers are against the idea of offering references before being asked, while others are of the opinion that you should offer. A good strategy is to wait until at least half of the interview to get a better understanding of how the interview is going. Generally, recruiters wouldn't ask for this information until the second or third round of the interviews. However, if you believe that the interview is going well, and you do believe yourself to be a good candidate for the job, then there is no harm in asking if they'd like to check your references. If you don't feel comfortable offering, then there is no harm in that either. If you are called for a second or third interview, the recruiter might e-mail you asking for them or request you to bring them with you to the interview. Either way, ALWAYS keep a few copies with you to be on the safe side.

Google Yourself and Fix it Up

According to a report by the Wall Street Journal, 85% of hiring managers 'Google' a candidate right after or sometimes before the interview. Online background checks have become a standard practice for businesses. And while negative information could get you in trouble, no information about you would not get you any brownie points either. In current times, it is imperative to have a presence online, and in order to land a good job, that presence needs to be clean and desirable. But what if you have a common name and Google doesn't show a lot of results for your name? Or worst what if you share the same name with some notorious leader or celebrity? According to a survey by Harris Interactive, 48% of people who Google themselves claim the results weren't very positive. Following are a few tips and tactics to clean up your Google image:

Sign out of your Google account before searching for yourself. Also, try turning off locations or search through an incognito window so that your search results aren't user or area-specific. This will show up non-custom results.

What do you see in the results? Would you hire you? Even a small tiff about political views or racial comments could ring warning bells for the recruiters, so make the conflicts disappear. Check your social media profiles. And this not only means your LinkedIn profile should look clean and professional, but your profiles on other social networking sites like Facebook, Instagram, and Twitter should give off positive vibes. Do not overdo it. Your social networking sites are, after all your personal space, and they should seem as such. While a butt-naked video on Instagram might seem questionable, you don't want passport photographs, resumes, and appreciation certificates pasted everywhere either. Fortunately, you can control what others see on Google about you. Visit Google's privacy center or go to aboutme.google.com and control the amount of information about you that Google can share. However, this only means that the information would be hidden from Google search results, but would still be available on the internet. Recruiters know their way around and would likely be thorough with their searches. So better do your homework and prefer removing any red flags rather than trying to hide them.

Check the images section on Google also. Do you see pictures of yourself there? And do you like them? Is there a particular picture you feel could put you in a bad light? Get to the source of it and remove it.

Chapter 2: Assessing Yourself

Doing self-assessment before interviews can assist you in making decisions about jobs by defining your skills, interests, values, achievements, strengths, and weaknesses. Employers today have many qualified candidates from which to choose. You will only be considered for a position if you can demonstrate that you know who you are and how your set of qualifications and personal qualities can benefit their company. Through the process of self-assessment, you will be able to decide what contributions you can take to the marketplace. By becoming more self-aware, you will improve your confidence and your ability to directly answer questions about your qualifications and experience.

To find out about yourself, you will have to reflect on your past experiences and personality and think of ways to articulate this information to the interviewer in a proper manner. One of the key questions you have to answer during the self-assessment phase is – What makes you a suitable candidate that stands out from the crowd. Answering this question can be distilled down to 2 simple steps:

1) Identify Your Skills – Start off by creating a list on a piece of paper of what you believe you are good at. Do this by reviewing your current and previous jobs and listing particular career skills you have gained, put them under different topics headings.

List what you have achieved to date and those points you feel you did well in and can demonstrate, give examples of and also prove. A good way to start will be create 3 broad categories – "previous experience", "portable skills" and "personality", and start filling in these 3 columns with qualities or skills that you can relate to. By the end of 30 minutes to an hour, you should have the quite a portion of the columns filled up.

2) Filtering the Skills – In the next step, you want to ensure that you highlight the skills or characteristics which may resonate with the hirer. Look at the job description and read it carefully, look for keywords that describe the skills and capabilities that an employer is expecting from an applicant. Then build and develop your resume or cover letter around the relevant skills that are required. If you can demonstrate to an employer that you have the qualities and capabilities they are looking for then you have a good chance of being successful in moving on to the next round. You might also want to think about how these qualities you possess can help to add value to a team within the company. For example, you might want to talk about how your past experience in product management will allow you to integrate into the team seamlessly. You can also talk about how resourceful and creative you are by proposing interesting ways to improve the efficiency of a team or the company. If you are able to accomplish all these, there is a great chance that you can stand out from the crowd and be remembered by the interviewer at the end of the session.

Ultimately, you want to make use of this self-assessment to better your odds of nailing that interview. In addition to that, you will also want to create a good resume or CV to showcase your capabilities.

Here is a tip to making a great CV: Quantify your impact. Avoid using vague terms such as "improve this" or "managed that". Show your accomplishments in numbers, not just words. A good example will be "Oversaw a 50% improvement in system efficiency within 4 weeks of taking on project."

Chapter 3: How To Prepare Yourself For A Job Interview?

Before getting yourself prepared for an interview, you must have to understand- What is an interview?

The interview is actually a two-way lane with both you and the interviewer taking an active role. It is primarily an opportunity to take a positive step on your career path. Your previous experience or education is not enough to convince an employer that you are the right person for the right job.

The outcome of a job interview is entirely dependent on how well you sell yourself.

What's the purpose of an interview?

Remember, everything has a reason in life, including your interview. An interview is the employer's way of selecting the right candidate from the bunch of equally-qualified candidates. Perhaps, you can say that an interview is an elimination process, wherein the winner receives a job letter.

What can be the objectives of an interview?

The main objectives of an interview can be;

The employer wants to know if you're a good fit for his/her company. The interviewer/HR Deptt is interested in knowing 3 things:

Are you able do the job?

Are you willing to do the job?

Will you fit in?

From the prospect of candidate; you want to sell yourself as an ideal candidate and you want to know if the company is suitable for you and your career goals.

An interview is interviewer's opportunity to match your skills and experience directly with the position he has offered.

What are your strengths?

What are your weaknesses?

How are you suitable for this job?

How long do you plan to stay with the company?

What is your ideal position?

Why do you want to change jobs?

Whereas an interview is also your opportunity to assess the company:

Is this the kind of place where you want to work?

Can you contribute?

Will you acquire new skills?

Is there a possibility to advance?

Will this position open doors for you?

What to do BEFORE an Interview? How do YOU prepare YOURSELF for an interview?

Here are some things to do the day before an interview. Remember, first impressions usually last!

Collect information about the company. Visit Website, Check LinkedIn page of the company. Gather as much information about company as you can.

Prepare what you plan to bring with you to the interview (including a list of references).

Prepare what you're going to wear (Be selective while choosing formals with proper matching).

Prepare for the interview questions, including topics about your;

work experience

academic history

skills and abilities

knowledge of the organization

career goals and objectives

accomplishments and achievements

personal and motivational factors

money and salary

Well, rehearse your responses in front of a mirror, or role play with another person or may be with your friend.

Practice your introduction.

Make sure you have the company's present address and the correct directions to go.

Make your transportation arrangements ahead of time.

BE PUNCTUAL! (utmost important)

What to do DURING an Interview?

Make Your Entrance

Before you say your first word, the interviewer will make a judgment about you. Remember, you might be on CCTV the moment you entered the office, so watch your action and body language. Be polite and professional when you speak to receptionist. There are a few key things that they will be looking for, including: a genuine smile, a firm handshake, a confident demeanor, good eye contact, and a friendly, enthusiastic introduction. They'll notice instantly whether your hair is clean and neat, whether or not your attire is appropriate, whether or not your breath is fresh, and if your hands and fingernails are clean.

Knock before you open the door.

Stick out your hand confidently.

Smile.

Relax and breathe deeply.

Be natural.

Speak slowly and clearly.

But, Remember: Don't get too comfortable!

Attitude Counts: This is the time to show off your interpersonal skills.

Interviewers are looking for key character traits and you need to demonstrate them at the interview.

Keep the following things in your mind:

Listening Skills: good listening skills and a pleasant demeanor are key attributes in any job.

Make sure you let the interviewer complete his sentence, don't interrupt him/her in between.

Show interest in what he/she says. Encourage him/her to talk and ask questions where it required.

Speak and sit with confidence. The quality of your interview presentation are the keys to its success

Silence. (Do you get rattled easily?)

Enthusiasm: you need to demonstrate to the interviewer that:

You are extremely interested in the position.

Remember, enthusiasm is contagious and interviewers are always keen to add members to their team. Your positive attitude will also rub off on the others as long as it is genuine and not overplayed and he will leave the interview with favorable "feel" about you.

Eye Contact:

Maintain eye contact with the interviewer. Looking away continuously suggests distractibility and disinterest.

Looking down makes you appear insecure and shy.

By all means, keep it natural. Feel free to nod your head, smile, and even laugh (where appropriate).

Flexibility:

You need to demonstrate to the interviewer that you are willing and able to adapt readily to new environments, demands, personas styles, etc.

Professionalism:

Above all, be PROFESSIONAL! Respect the interviewer. Remember the interview boundaries at all times, don't behave in an either overly-casual fashion or overly-aggressive manner with the interviewer.

What to do AFTER Interview is over?

Congratulations! You made it through the interview!

What's the next step?

Wait for the company to respond to you.

Nagging them with phone calls and visits is annoying and completely unprofessional behavior.

Follow up and phone the company a week or ten days later inquiring about the status of the job vacancy.

If you get rejected for the job, consider it a valuable learning experience.

Interview Do's and Don'ts

There are some basic tips and strategies to be aware of while being interviewed.

The basic thumb rules are:

Dos:

Have a positive tone.

Be prepared to face difficult questions.

Collect information about the company before the interview.

Focus on what you have to offer to a prospective interviewer, not what you want.

Think about what you can do for the interviewer/company.

Follow up with a note and/or phone call.

Look directly at the interviewer.

Elaborate briefly on your experience, your skills, and background.

Be sincere.

Be natural, allowing your sense of humor show.

Think before you answer. It is quite acceptable to pause before responding in order to organize your thoughts.

Be a good listener. Ask for clarification if you're not sure about what's being asked.

Be calm and poised.

Be aware of your nervous habits, and try to keep them under control.

Shut the door on your troubles. Never discuss your troubles. Avoid discussions about family or financial problems.

Say good-bye to the receptionist. Being polite may provide you with the extra edge you needed to close the interview.

Don't

Lie on your resume.

Plead/beg for a job!

Exaggerate or compare yourself to others.

Cross your arms across your chest. This gesture will make you seem defensive.

Place anything on the desk between you and the interviewer, such as your laptop or portfolio. It can be misinterpreted as a barrier.

Give just "yes" and "no" answers. One-liners are conversation stoppers.

Use flattery, an interviewer will recognize flattery and consider you insincere.

Argue with the interviewer.

Criticize your old job or boss.

Speak too loudly or too softly.

Do not comment on politics, religious other controversial topics.

Don't start interviews with your fingers crossed hoping that they "give you the job" nobody is going to "give you the job".

Talk about money in the first interview.

It is greatly said, "Fear doesn't shut you down, it wakes you up!"

No doubt interviews and interviewers alike can be fearful, but overcoming them is your key to grabbing success. So, have full confidence in you and I really hope that you believe in yourselves, and smash your interview and yes, always remember that "Everything that you've ever wanted is on the other side of fear."

Chapter 4: Use Technology Wisely

Technology is a major part of our lives. Some people even spend more time within their e-life instead their real one. Having said that living in an era that everyone is using a mobile phone, tablet, notebook, PCs and everyone has at least one or several electronic profiles such as Facebook, LinkedIn, MySpace, Twitter and so on, is very easy to use the technology to find out more information about a person. As you have established your research about finding which companies in your area are interested in hiring people with your skills and knowledge, with the same exact way the company you have applied for will search the web in order to find out more information about you. And when we say "you" we do not mean that the company will do it just for you personally but the same process will be used for all applicants applied for the job position. This way the company can find out information (some negative and some positive) for the applicants and filter out the resumes according to that.

So what you need to do? You need to update and adjust your e-life and phone voice mail in order not to give out any faulty or negative impressions to the people that will search out for you.

•Mobile Device: Start with your mobile ring song / music. It is a common practice that some people will adopt a song or theme music for others to hear when dial their numbers. In case you have a service like that enabled on your phone will be strongly suggested to disabling it. Not everyone share the same style and type of music or it may happen that your favorite song brings out bad memories to the HR manager who is assigned to give you a call and schedule your interview. Guess what will happen if this is the case? You guessed it right! They will hang up on you and there goes your opportunity to that position.

•Voice Mail: Create a voice mail that demonstrates confidence and professionalism. Avoid having any messages with jokes or offending comments. If you have created your current voice mail while driving and people can hear all the traffic noise and cars horning in the background then you should consider create a new message without any background noise. A professional and proper voice mail will be something as below: "Hello. You have reached the voice mail of Christos Minterides. I am not able to take your phone call at the moment but if you leave your name and phone number will contact you as soon as possible. Thank you."

- E-mail Address: It is common that most of us have multiple e-mail addresses that we use in our daily lives. We have one for our friends to contact us, one for our family and so on. For the job interview process and for your business career you should create an email such as:

- Internet Activity / E-Profiles: If you are a person that enjoys activities indoors or outdoors and you like living life to the fullest and at the same time you love making memories of these moments by taking a lot of photos and then sharing with your friends online then you should sit down and filter them

out. Photos in your personal profile of you drinking beers and dancing on the roof of the house will not give you any positive points. You could switch your Facebook account so that only your close friends could access your profile and content.

- NO NO: Avoid any controversial comments and postings about politics, religion or any other hot topics. These are a big NO NO and you should avoid them.

Chapter 5: The Basics Of Sales

Sales, like many things in life, can be learned in a day yet it takes a lifetime to master. But the good news for you is that, unless you are interviewing for a highly competitive sales position, you are not likely competing against people who have mastered sales. You are competing against people who are merely going to dress nice, smile real big and hope that their resume is the winning resume. The sales process is a very simple formula.

Prospecting

Preparation

Presentation

Discovery

Solution

Closing

Follow up

That's it. It is just five steps. Variations of this model exist for different industries and situations. But they are essentially the same. It's a simple process. For many sales situations the process is a circle that continues around and around. For a job interview, a linear progression from start to finish seems more appropriate. Take some time now and memorize the steps. A good salesperson always knows where they are in the sales process.

We will spend the rest of the book discussing how to maximize your efforts in each step. Before we start here is some more good news. If you already have an interview scheduled with a company you have already completed the prospecting step! Only four steps remain.

The prospecting step consists of preparing your resume, finding various companies with job openings, determining which jobs you want to apply for, tailoring your resume for each position and applying for the jobs. Now that you have an interview/s it is time to move on to the next stage.

Chapter 6: "First Impressions"

Question 1: What were your responsibilities?

When you are asked questions related to your current or previous positions, it's important to be specific and to be positive about what you did in your previous position(s).

The best way to respond is to describe your responsibilities in detail and to connect them to the job for which you are interviewing.

Try to tie your responsibilities in with those listed in the job description for the new position.

That way, the employer will see that you have the qualifications necessary to do the job.

Focus most on your responsibilities that are directly related to the new job's requirements. It's also important to be honest. Don't embellish your job because you don't know with whom the hiring manager will be checking when he/she checks your references.

Question 2: What did you like or dislike about your previous job?

When you're asked what you don't like about your previous job, don't be too negative. You don't want the interviewer to think that you'll speak negatively about the new job or the company when you're ready to move on, if you get this job. Rather, it makes sense to talk about yourself and what you're looking for in a new role.

Question 3: What were your starting and final levels of compensation?

Interviewers expect a candidate for employment to be able to provide the details of their compensation history.

Be prepared to tell the interviewer how much you earned at each of your prior positions.

Make sure that what you tell the interviewer matches what you listed on your job application.

Refresh your memory prior to the interview by reviewing your salary history so you can speak in detail and accurately.

Don't exaggerate or inflate your earnings. Many employers will check references and confirm your salary history prior to making a job offer.

A discrepancy between what you reported and what your previous employer says could knock you out of contention for the job.

Question 4: What major challenges and problems did you face? How did you handle them?

When asked the job interview question "How did you handle a challenge?", be sure to include specific examples of how you handled a particular difficult situation.

Discuss how you researched the issue and contributed to finding a solution.

Question 5: What is your greatest strength?

"What is your greatest strength?" is one of the easier interview questions you'll be asked. When you are asked questions about your strengths, it's important to discuss attributes that will qualify you for the job.

The best way to respond is to describe the skills and experience that directly correlate with the job for which you are applying.

Question 6: What is your greatest weakness?

When asked what your greatest weakness is, one option is try to turn a negative into a positive.

For example, a sense of urgency to get projects completed or wanting to triple-check every item in a spreadsheet can be turned into a strength; i.e., you are a candidate who will make sure that the project is done on time and your work will be close to perfect.

Question 7: How do you handle stress and pressure?

Think hard before you answer this one. If you are not comfortable in stressful situations, be honest and explain how you deal with it. If you thrive under pressure, expound on that.

Examples of good responses include:

"I react to situations, rather than to stress. That way, the situation is handled and doesn't become stressful."

"I actually work better under pressure and I've found that I enjoy working in a challenging environment."

"I find a past pace to be invigorating and thrive when the pressure is on."

"I've done some of my best work under tight deadlines where the atmosphere was very stressful."

"I'm the kind of person who stays calm under pressure and handles stress fairly easily."

"From a personal perspective, I manage stress by visiting the gym every evening. It's a great stress reducer."

Question 8: Describe a difficult work situation / project and how you overcame it.

There is no right or wrong answer to questions like "What are the most difficult decisions to make?" or "Describe a difficult work situation / project and how you overcame it."

These are behavioural interview questions designed to discover how you handled certain situations.

The logic behind these types of questions is that how you behaved in the past is a predictor of what you will do in the future.

Give concrete examples of difficult situations that actually happened at work.

Then discuss what you did to solve the problem. Keep your answers positive.

Question 9: What was the biggest accomplishment / failure in this position?

Your potential employer will want to know what you accomplished and what you didn't in your current or last position.

The best way to respond is to give an example of something you accomplished that is directly related to the job for which you are interviewing.

Review your resume and review the job posting.

Find the best match and use that to show how what you accomplished will be beneficial to the company with which you are interviewing.

If you didn't fail at anything, say so. If you can think of an example, be sure that it's a minor one and turn it into a positive.

Question 10: How do you evaluate success?

This is another behavioural question where there is no right or wrong answer.

Think about the best answer for you and practice your response.

The interviewer is trying to get a sense of your values. Be honest and give an example of an example of what you find to be successful.

Question 11: Why are you leaving or have left your job?

This can be a tricky question and should be handled with thought. If you left on your own accord, be honest and explain why.

If you were fired or let go, be honest, but turn the negative connotation into a positive.

For example, "Being let go was a blessing in disguise. Now I can apply myself to something I am really good at."

Keep your answer simple and keep moving so you can address the new job possibilities and talk about why you are qualified for this job.

Question 12: Why do you want this job?

This question is often the most difficult to answer off the cuff. Be sure to think about it and prepare your answer.

Be honest and sincere and take this as another opportunity to sell your skills and talents.

Question 13: Why should we hire you?

The best way to respond is to give concrete examples of why your skills and accomplishments make you the best candidate for the job.

Take a few moments to compare the job description with your abilities, as well as mentioning what you have accomplished in your other positions.

Be positive and reiterate your interest in the company and the position.

This is an opportunity to give your opinion and validate the interviewer's opinion on why you are the best candidate for the job.

Question 14: What are your goals for the future?

The best way to respond to this question is to refer to the position and the company with which you are interviewing.

Don't discuss your goals for returning to school or having a family.

These are not relevant and could knock you out of contention for the job.

Rather, you want to connect your answer to the job for which you are applying.

Question 15: What are your salary requirements?

Before you start talking pay (and salary negotiations) with a prospective employer, you need to find out how much the job (and you) is worth. You will need to take the time to research salaries. That way you will be prepared to get what you're worth and to get a job offer that's realistic and reasonable. Yellow Ribbon Reintegration Program **(MAR 2014) Acing the Interview** pg. 4

Question 16: Tell me about yourself.

Remember what we discussed in working on your 30-Second Commercial. This is the perfect time to use it!

Question 17: Who was your best boss and who was the worst?

The interviewer is trying to discover if you assess blame or carry a grudge. The interviewer also wants to determine if you are a match for the leadership style of the company. Be honest and be fair, but don't put down your former bosses. If you had an issue with someone in the past, address it professionally and don't make it personal.

Question 18: What are you passionate about?

When you're asked what you're passionate about during a job interview, it's a good opportunity to share what is important in your life. It's also an opportunity to show your dedication and why it is important to you. Your response doesn't need to be work focused, but be sure that what you share isn't something that could potential cut into your working hours.

Question 19: How do you balance work and life?

The interviewer wonders if you've made arrangements for the days when your child is too sick to go to school and/or daycare or if you're "out of there" as soon as it's quitting time. Be honest with your answer and if you have challenges, offer a solution of how you would handle it.

Question 20: What did you do during your six-month gap in employment?

Everyone, at some point, will probably have a gap in employment. Do not let the interviewer think you wasted your time. If you worked on "to do" lists, say so. Remember to include that you accomplished a lot. If you don't have a list of things you accomplished, you can talk about being well rested and ready to re-enter the work force.

Chapter 7: How To Stand Out In Today's Competitive Market

Whether you're consciously looking for a new job or being ready just in case, you're curious how to get your resume heard in today's competitive environment. So how do you stand out in a competitive sea-often equally qualified?

The solution is embedded by understanding the three must-haves to be included in your resume-By using the right job hunting techniques In this chapter, I would address the three must-haves for your resume.

First of all, when it comes to resuming, there are no tough and fast rules, as much of the strategy depends on the person and the situation. But we know that there are certain things that always work. Start by putting yourself in the shoes of a new worker or a recruiter. We see the remainder of the day full. They're just not going to sit there and read your 5-page essay-style resume. They're not going to try to break things together and figure out how your interesting and diverse background might fit into their organization. You need to make that clear to them.

Usually, they're going to spend about 10 seconds to see what's going on with them-specifically: who you are, what you do, where your skill is, and what you can do with them. In other terms, what kind of answer would you offer to their problem?

So here are my three must-haves that will allow your resume to be heard in your competition:

Your resume needs to be marked.

Private companies are a distinct pledge of quality. It's about what's best about you, which has a bottom line effect on a company. Once your resume is marked, it clarifies why you should be recruited above anyone else with the same experience, the same sort of roles, and even similar accomplishments. It's often about how you get the results. Employers want to learn how to do something new.

The personal brand is natural and authentic. It's really about who you are and your core skill set, and then distilled into a single, overriding factor that would make you irresistible to employers. It's also something that you'd have to do. The goal is to recognize and exploit it so that others can see it even more plainly.

How can you do this: it's not always easy to figure out your personal brand on your own as you're so close to the start. You should start by asking yourself-and those around you-what is it that you really do really well, that you want to do it, and that's of interest to the kind of boss you want to work with. It could be a couple things. It could be work-related, or it could be more of a personality thing. Or both of them. Once you've found your brand, you want to turn it into a max. 1-2 sentence branding statement. This is in the top third of your resume. And remember this: the companies are going to interview you for the money or the bottom line part of your brand. But they're going to hire you for the chemistry part. Nonetheless, you don't get through the door in the first place without the money part.

Your application needs to be targeted.

Trying to keep your options open on your application is almost always backfired. Also, mind that people take only a few seconds to check your resume. Nonetheless, don't use the hopelessly outdated "objective" because your application will concentrate on what you can do for your boss vs. what you want from them. Objectives typically read something like this: "Challenging place where I can leverage my skills and experience and have room for growth." These are vague assumptions and could be extended to anyone from a janitor to a CFO. So we want to create a clear focus to make it immediately clear who you are and what you do.

How can you do this?

When you remain in the same area, just bold your name (or variation) at the top of your resume. "Global Marketing Manager," "Senior Finance Director," "Executive Assistant," "Health Care Coordinator" or: Global Marketing Expert with 15 years of experience in product sectors.

If you want to pursue different styles of jobs in different industries, make sure you change your resume so that you have multiple versions. Just remember that an unfocused resume is an ineffective one. You can sound counter-intuitive if you're not sure what you want to do or if you want to keep your options open, but it's important to concentrate your resume.

Show proof of your claims.

In other words: back up the details of your product and company claim.

How can this be done? in the top section of your resume, build a rundown with a few lines max-don't go overboard-and tie either in quantifiable accomplishments or list one or two symbolic results that provide some sense (where you did this and with whom). This section is often referred to as a description or a profile. It doesn't matter what you call it, and there's no need for you to mark it on your resume. People are going to get what it's about. Stay away from a flowery fluff like "goal-oriented person with a track record in building relationships..." This is too simplistic and makes it look like everyone else's resume. Such assertions used to work, but they're no longer working. First, make sure to measure your accomplishments in your resume before explaining your achievements. Provide a context for them by comparing your achievements to industry or company averages, or to those of your peers or your predecessors. That way, the application doesn't feel like a job description. Instead, it will give readers a very clear picture of what unique things you've done and what sets you apart from John Doe with a similar background.

As a parting thought: Always make sure that everything on your resume is there for a reason and is relevant to your goal. The portfolio does not need to be all-inclusive. Anything that isn't important distracts from your core message. After all, you might have put together a really impressive resume, but if you're using poor job search techniques, you probably won't notice it. Job searching has endured some spectacular "nip and tuck" in the last few years. It's not just the market which renders the world more efficient. These days, your cv may not be the first item an organization can see from you. With the proliferation of social and business networking sites, it may be your profiles online.

So you need to learn how to design a resume, but you also need to know how to sell it and promote it yourself. At the end of the day, isn't it about businesses showing interest in you, whether it's through your resume or another medium? Many employers are going to Search you during the hiring process. They might even find you online to get going, or be directed to you by someone who has seen your profile online.

The good news is that you can be in the driver's seat by heading to the secret job market and using social networking. You definitely don't want to apply passively to positions that you see posted online. This has an overall success rate of 2 percent. For order to be truly effective for today's competitive job market, you need to use a mix of offline and digital networking. It's still great to network in person, and sometimes sending a hard copy of your resume will make you stand out at a time when email has become the norm. All kidding aside, whatever you do, you always want to make a connection or even a friendship. Even if this is through one of your connections. If you can have your resume turned over to a decision maker through a main link inside your target company; fantastic! That would have been perfect. When you go online, the emphasis should be on presenting yourself as an authority in your profession vs. requesting the network for a job. Social networking is perfect for that! You do this by posting on other people's blogs that are important to your area, by making your own blog and website — yes, a website! answering questions online, joining in group discussions and posting articles on your skills.

You also want to recognize hiring managers-not HR directors! -the businesses that you are involved in online so that you can contact them and hit them with your emails. After a while, you will be seen as an expert and a resource. Next, people may even approach you and refer you without asking, because you have established relationships within your network and provided value to others. It's important to make the error of asking people on your network for a position. They're in need, and most people don't have work to pass out. Which means: the end of the conversation. It's perfectly fine, though, to ask for leads for informational interviews.

With these techniques, you can also work more effectively on the invisible labor market. What this suggests is that you're going to find out about the company's recruiting requirements long before they're either promoted or published. But beware, when you're profiling online, you need to know your own brand. Otherwise, you're not going to stand out, or you might even send the wrong message about yourself.

Chapter 8: Closing Questions

If you were hired, what would you seek to accomplish in the first three months in the new job?

Employers ask this question to gauge how you think about ramping up on your new role, how fast you are going to complete the on-boarding process, and the types of standards and goals you have set for yourself, especially it being a new environment.

Remember that this time is also when you will be learning a lot about your responsibilities, your leaders, as well as the workplace etiquette. You will be adjusting and learning how to fit into the larger organization.

A part of your own interview preparation should be understanding what the particular job responsibilities and company structure will be like and to align it with your goals in order to ace this question.

Clearly, the longer it would take you to contribute significantly to the organization, the less admirable you would be. Therefore, avoid being vague or showing how you will probably still be adapting to the new environment. Employers today are interested in the fast-paced, innovative, and easily adaptable personnel.

A good answer would be, for instance, besides getting to know the team and fully tuning to the role, there is a lot more I'd like to accomplish in the first three months. In the first month, I want to learn the design of our marketing projects. After two months, I want to redesign and launch a project by tuning the efforts of the team, and after three months, I want to be able to track the growth of our marketing efforts.

What questions haven't I asked you?

Employers make this inquiry to assess your interest in the field and your enthusiasm and commitment to improving yourself as a worker in the industry. It offers a chance to showcase your ability to decipher information and establish anything you feel is important that they have not touched. Pointing out such a thing is what sets you apart and shows that you know what brought you here, how different you are, and your planned contributions.

Naturally, a person to be considered will be the one who seems truly invested in the industry and their personal development.

Be sure to emphasize your stage of career development, how you want to develop yourself professionally, and your long-term goals.

Avoid arrogance like showing you are the pinnacle of development with nothing extra to learn. Do not emphasize your idealized salary and fun job.

You could say, for instance, my main focus is to continue developing my leadership and organizational skills, and I believe in constantly challenging myself to achieve more. My vision is around the big picture, and I want to exploit that ability the best possible way.

What questions do you have for me?

As the interview comes to a close, the interviewer is most likely to ask if you have any questions for them. It may feel as if you have covered everything in the course of your interview, but it is paramount to respond to this question rather than decline.

Your response should be guided by the knowledge of with whom you are interviewing. If it is your potential manager, then you can ask questions about the responsibilities of the position. If it is human resource personnel, however, you can ask questions generally about the organization.

You should prepare a list of various questions to ask during this phase in case some of them are addressed during the interview. Your response to this question will tell how keen you were during the conversation.

About the company you can ask:

Can you talk a bit about the company culture?

What are the goals of the company for the upcoming year?

About the role you can ask:

Could you please share more about the daily routine responsibilities of the job?

What is the major indicator of accomplishment in this job, from your perspective?

Avoid questions on topics such as off-work activities, interviewer's personal life, minor things you could answer yourself, as well as salary and benefits.

Would you work holidays and weekends?

Simple as it looks, this question can effectively set aside individuals to be hired and those to be rejected. Some industries require workers to be flexible and be able to juggle work and other commitments because of frequent projects or long hours of operation needed at times.

Some tips when answering this question include being realistic about your time, but give your response a positive spin. For instance, you can say, I have no problem working on weekends or holidays as long as I can schedule myself as early as possible.

Also, know your limits. Employers need confidence in a candidate who can keep time commitments. For instance, you can say, due to family commitments, I cannot commit to working every weekend and every holiday, but I can certainly give some of the days if need be.

You do not want to say a flat no and give your interviewer the impression that you cannot give up some of your free time for work purposes. Industries such as hospitality require this element.

Ideally, show some flexibility in your schedule, indicate that you have time management skills, and be confident and tactful. Avoid committing to a schedule that you cannot keep, and do not disclose more information about your schedule than necessary.

How would you fire someone?

This counter-intuitive question is raised especially when you are looking for a management position. The recruiter wants to assess if you have really got what it takes. Are you able to deliberate and fire an employee when necessary or just ignore the problem? Also, they are concerned that you will fire someone in a way that upholds the rights of the company and confidentiality of the employee when firing them.

Take this opportunity to demonstrate your management style and re-emphasize the leadership skills (such as emotional intelligence) you expressed in earlier parts of the interview. Show that you would never take firing someone lightly.

Avoid being mean when role-playing, as it is not the time to channel your perceived inner strength. Rather, respectfully show that you are firm and ready to make reasons for firing clear.

A reasonable way to fire is to say something like, I'd first of all try to see if there is anything I can do to prevent having to fire the individual, such as constant communication and performance review. If it comes to the point that I have to terminate their contract, I'd engage with them privately without the knowledge of any other employee and explain the reason for termination.

Chapter 9: Situational Interview Questions

Situational interview questions ask job applicants to imagine a set of conditions and then specify how they would respond in that situation; hence, the questions are future oriented. One advantage of situational questions is that all interviewees respond to the same hypothetical situation rather than describe experiences unique to them from their past. Another advantage is that situational questions allow respondents who have had no direct job experience relevant to a particular question to provide a hypothetical response. Two core aspects of the SI are the development of situational dilemmas that employees encounter on the job, and a scoring guide to evaluate responses to each dilemma.

Situational examples

You are in charge of truck drivers in Toronto. Your colleague is in charge of truck drivers in Montreal. Both of you report to the same person. Your salary and bonus are affected 100% by your costs. Your colleague is in desperate need of one of your trucks. If you say no, your costs will remain low and your group will probably win the Golden Flyer award for the quarter. If you say yes, the Montreal group will probably win this prestigious award because they will make a significant profit for the company. Your boss is preaching costs, costs, costs, as well as co-operation with one's peers. Your boss has no control over accounting who are the score keepers. Your boss is highly competitive; he or she rewards winners. You are just as competitive; you are a real winner! What would you do in this situation?

You are in a meeting. Your manager blames you for not doing well on a task, in front of all your peers and managers from other divisions. You believe that your manager is wrong in his critique, and that he might have come to this conclusion hastily without knowing all the information. You feel you are being treated unfairly in front of your peers. You feel that your reputation may be affected by this critique. What would you do in this situation?

You are managing a work group and notice that one of your employees has become angry and hostile in recent weeks, to the point of disrupting the entire group. What would you do?

A general request has been issued by the Dean for someone to serve on a new joint government/industry/university
committee on business education. The objective of the committee is to design the budgeting allocation for the Faculty for the next fiscal year. It is well known that you have the necessary skill and expertise to improve the chances that the Faculty will receive budget increases for future operations. You have been told that it will require 2–3 days per month of your time for the next 9 months. Your tenure review

is one year away. Although you think you have a good publication record, you have no guarantee of tenure at this point. You are concerned because you have already fallen behind on an important research project that you are pursuing with a colleague at another university. What, if anything, would you do?

Chapter 10: Top Job Interview Questions

If you ended up working for somebody who was less knowledgeable than you, how would you handle it?

Working for somebody who knows less than you can be frustrating and difficult. However, it's infrequent that they're less knowledgeable then you on every single topic. And generally, there is a reason why they are higher up than you. They clearly have more knowledge than you somewhere to have gotten that position. Even if there's nothing you can learn from them despite the fact that they're in charge, you need to help them succeed. Generally if you help them reach their goals, they will help you reach yours as well. However, in an interview, what they really want to know is whether or not you can accept that fact that some people are more knowledgeable than you, and it is also important that you learn something from them.

Some personality types have a tougher time with this, and it's also a problem with older employees (over 50) who believe they don't have anything to learn from the younger crowd. If you're interviewing as an older individual, keep this stereotype in mind. You need to do everything possible to avoid it, so don't criticize the generation below you or complain about a stupid 20-something you worked with. It will only hurt you, even if you're right and the kid was dumber than a brick.

This question is searching for a weakness. It's just another question trying to figure out how you handle stress. They want to know if you will react negatively, so do your best to avoid that. Many people will be hired to work for people younger than them. Some people don't care either way, and it's usually pretty obvious to the hiring manager during the interview. These people respond with something along the lines of "In my experience, even people who are less knowledge than me in one area tend to be more knowledgeable than me in another. In this case, we can both learn from each other and it makes the process enjoyable for everybody." Other people take on a more snarky approach and respond with something like "It can be frustrating, but I try to show them how it's done without seeming like a threat". It sounds positive, but it really isn't. Generally, something like that makes the interviewer dislike you because they would hate to be the one leading your team, and before you know it the job offer is gone.

What would you do to prove your credibility to the team?

The easiest way to prove your credibility anywhere, with anyone, is to ask good questions and gain a solid understanding of the situation before you do anything about it. This is also why it's important to ask good questions during an interview - it gives you a chance to show that you know what to ask. Good questions will make you seem like a credible and viable candidate to the interviewer.

It's a common misconception that the best way to handle a bad situation is by charging in and fixing it right away. However, in most cases this will only lead to mistakes and make you look arrogant. It also doesn't help when it comes to building relationships with others. The best thing to start with is asking questions that reveal your knowledge of the situation. With this information, you can make a better decision rather than leaping in unprepared. However, there are some situations where actions are more important than words and the best way to establish yourself is to get to work right away and do everything you can to help. Thanks to this, this question is a great spot to tell the interviewer all about your 30-60-90 plan. Respond with: "The best way for me to answer this question is to tell you about my outline of what I hope to accomplish during my first three months with you. Do you mind going over my plan with me?" If they agree, impress the hiring manager with every aspect of your plan.

In case you've never heard of this before, a 30-60-90 day plan outlines the actions you will take in your first three months on the job in order to acclimate to your new position. This plan requires extensive research on both the job and the company, because it is even more impressive if it is specific. The research also helps make you the most knowledgeable and well-prepared candidate. The plan displays your capability, even if you don't have very much experience with that particular job. It shows your strategic thinking skills, your ability to prioritize tasks and analyze situations, and your willingness to go the distance. The plan itself and your description of it both show the interviewer that you are the type to get involved, establish yourself, and then serve as a successful leader of member of the team.

This position is not as high up as some of your previous ones. Why are you investigating jobs that are basically a demotion?

This questions tends to come earlier on in the process, generally during the phone interview stages. If your history shows that you have extensive experience, it will be obvious to the interviewer that you are overqualified. Naturally, they want to know why you're taking a job that is below what you could be working and earning. Of the many responses you have, the very, very last one should be that you're desperate for work. Even if you're at risk of losing your house and your savings have run dry, never say so. Companies are always worried that the people they're interviewing will take any job they can grab at the moment, which makes them more likely to run off to something better once the chance comes along.

Another common concern is that the new hire will be bored in this less interesting job, which means it isn't a good fit, which means they'll become unhappy and probably leave. This is a waste of their time, money, and training, so they want to hear that this job is the one you really want. In our ultra competitive society, working a job that doesn't use your potential to its fullest is often seen as unusual, but in reality there are many reasons to take a step back.

Perhaps this new company requires an easier commute, or maybe you climbed the ladder to management but discovered the lower hands-on aspect to be more interesting. Maybe you prefer this company's mission and products, or maybe it offers a unique experience that can't be found elsewhere, or maybe its culture is better for your personality. Maybe your old job was with a smaller company that had fewer opportunities for advancement, so you decided to take a step back into a bigger company with more opportunities. These are all good reasons, but none of them are immediately apparent to the interviewer. Make sure to tell them exactly why this newer, albeit lower, position is the better match for you. Let them know that your experience actually helps them because they will benefit from it. Also, you will likely be a step above other candidates, which gives you a boost and another way to sell yourself to the interviewer. Make sure they take notice!

If we decide to take you into our team, picture yourself here a year from now. What new things will we have learned about you?

This, along with "tell me about yourself", is a question that is easy to get sidetracked on. When talking about yourself, you don't want to venture into your love of soccer, your excellent bean chili recipe, or your reluctance to use sick days. Stay focused, and use this question as another opportunity to sell yourself to the interviewer. Every single interview question should be used to get you closer and closer to an offer. Every answer should give them information about you, but not just any information. It should tell them why you are perfect for the job. It should make them want to hire you on the spot.

Every answer must be strategized, and this one's role is to give them an idea of what you working there would look like. If you can help them visualize it, you will be one step closer to an offer. When you go furniture shopping, you picture the item in your house, right? You imagine what it would be like to sit there with your dog or read your favorite book or watch the game. The more you picture it in your life, the more likely you are to make the purchase. In an interview, you want them to picture you in the position you want. This is also one of the reasons why 30-60-90 day plans are so effective.

This question is intended to help the hiring manager see you in the job. Personally, I enjoy using "If I work here, a year from now I will have proven everything I told you during this interview true." They'll likely ask you to elaborate, and you can then explain that they'll understand why all of your previous employers liked having you around and wished they could have you back. (On this note, don't forget the importance of references. They are an incredible resource that you should always take advantage of, so always make sure that yours are prepared for any phone calls that may come their way).

Or you could say something like "You'll know that I'm being honest when I say how excited I am to learn more about this company and this job. You'll also know that I fully intend on thriving here, contributing to this company, and producing to my fullest extent during my time as your [job position]." If you want to be specific, tell them how they'll know that your skill set was a perfect match for the position, then detail the skills and how you have proven them before. Overall, this question is yet another version of "why should we hire you?". Make sure that they know you will meet and maybe exceed their hopes for you.

When it comes to collaborative projects, how do you handle a team member who does not contribute their fair share?

One of the more common questions posed to interested applicants during a job interview is whether or not they have had any problems with working with others in the past, especially when it comes to projects that require close collaboration. This question is loved by interviewers for a very good reason. After all, who doesn't remember having some deadweight in their group back in school? In addition, almost any job you'll be applying for will require you to work together with your colleagues on one or more projects. In light of this, it's almost unavoidable that this question will be asked in one form or another.

When the time inevitably comes for you to come up with an answer, remember to be careful when phrasing your reply. Remember that nobody likes a whiner, and even though you may not be the one holding the group back, it will reflect negatively on you if you are perceived to be whiny. One suggestion for answering this question is to focus on what you were able to contribute in order to pick up the slack, rather than complaining about it. After all, when the situation arises, it is best to focus on your part and when done, maybe then you can begin work on the portion of the slacker. If you work this way, that is the best thing to say to the interviewer. Telling them that you focused on getting your work done, then went to the supervisor or the team leader in order to assist them with finding a solution for making up for the non-contributing member sounds far better than telling them that you reported the culprit, or that you simply confronted them. Another possible response could be that you offered to assist the person in question, as you know that everyone working together is the key to the team's success. The crucial point when responding is to get the message across that you remain focused on getting your work done, and that you are a team player. If you badmouth people behind their backs, even if they did something wrong, it shows you to be unprofessional, and your interviewer will wonder if you will do it to them if you get the job. Remember that one of the best interview strategies is to keep things positive rather than negative.

Have you encountered problems when dealing with your superiors at work?

Let's face it. It's very likely that at one point or another during our careers, we will end up working under someone who doesn't treat us like we should be treated, or is ineffective in their role. Remember, however, when the interviewer asks us about these people, this is not an invitation to rant about that time when your former boss did that thing. Rather, this is one of the ways that an interviewer tries to get to know you better. Asking about how you dealt with a superior you didn't like helps them find out how you are as an employee or co-worker. If you choose to rant, then they will simply think that you are someone who complains a lot and is fond of badmouthing people. If you talk about how your former supervisor played favorites, the interviewer will just assume you are bitter and may be a bad co-worker. If you complain that your old boss didn't appreciate how you worked, then the interviewer may simply think that you may really just didn't work hard enough.

Be cautious when you answer this question, as even legitimate concerns with some of your former bosses may be taken the wrong way if you speak about them to the interviewer. Remember that interviews should remain positive rather than negative. One possible response to the question is to say that you never really ran into any major problems with your former bosses. You could further elaborate by saying that different people have different managerial styles, and there is a lot to learn from each one of them. This answer points to you being adaptable and willing to work and compromise. If ever there is a story that has to be told, try and portray it as positively as possible. For example, you could tell a story about how your former supervisor gave you a hard time all the time in a different manner. You could say that "I started off with the wrong foot when I started working in my old job, as my supervisor and I had differing expectations from my work. I was inexperienced at the time, so I didn't immediately realize that. However, I was advised to talk to him, and we were able to clear the air and move forward. I was able to learn much from that, one of the lessons being that opening proper channels of communication is the key to developing a good relationship." When you tell the story like that, you aren't saying anything bad about either one of you, but rather talking about how the situation gave both of you a hard time. In fact, you were even able to be mature about it and solved the problem.

What particular set of skills do you have that can contribute to improving the company's growth and development?

If ever the interviewer is asking you this question, then it's quite likely that you are already applying for a higher position, perhaps a managerial or even an executive role. When you are asked this question, you have to keep in mind what exactly your role will be if ever, and you have to be very specific when it comes to answering just what exactly you will be able to contribute to the company. Remember, this is a higher-level position and they are not looking for a warm body, but rather someone who can take a leadership role. You have to impress upon them the reasons why they should you be hiring you versus your competitors, and one of the best ways to get them to realize this is to be prepared. At the outset, you should be able to prepare three or even four ways that you and your set of skills would benefit the company, meaning that preparing for this requires extensive research. In fact, if you are even able to prepare a thirty-sixty-ninety day plan, then you will score bonus points and will most likely be the standout candidate, showing them how much thought and preparation you've put into the role.

Even if you are not being interviewed for a higher position, this question remains relevant. No matter what role you will be taking in the company, there is a value to it; otherwise the position would not exist. Every role in a company has a purpose, and that is to make the company profitable, one way or another, directly or through playing a supporting role. When you answer the question, remember that any role, no matter how menial or lowly it may seem, plays a part in the company's success. A janitor helps with revenue by cleaning the location and making customers feel more comfortable and welcome, or allowing employees to be more productive due to a cleaner workspace. A waitress in a diner is not a robot serving food, but rather represents the diner to its customers, maybe even being the key factor in whether the customer will be a repeat one or will badmouth the place to their friends. Keep this in mind whenever you answer this question, and as long as you know what role your prospective job plays in the company's framework, then you will be able to ace this particular query.

Chapter 11: How To Search For An Interview Opportunity

Remember as you search job postings that you aren't just looking for jobs to apply to. You are looking for an interview opportunity. Applying for the job is just the first step.

In order to really show a potential employer what you are capable of and why you are the right person for the job, you have to get in front of them. A face to face interview is the best way to sell yourself to the employer. And that is exactly what you have to do. You have to sell them on the idea that you can do the job better than anyone else.

In order to land an interview you have to have an amazing application. This means that your resume must be complete and well organized, as well as free from spelling and grammar mistakes. It must list not only your work experience and education, but your accomplishments, skills and talents as well.

The most important part of your application for any job is your cover letter. Your cover letter is your first impression. It is how you will stand apart from other candidates. Your cover letter has to shout to the employer, "Look at me! I'm the best for the job!"

The way you do this through a cover letter is to apply what you know about yourself to what you know about the position and the company. When you link these two things together in a positive way, you make the employer think positively about you as a candidate.

If the company's application process does not include the ability to attach a cover letter, send one in a follow up email. Send an email to the human resources department of the company letting them know that you have applied, and include everything that you would normally send in a cover letter. This lets the company know that you are serious about your application for the position, and gives you the opportunity to sell yourself for an interview.

You should also follow up on this email or your application within a few days with a phone call to the human resources department of the company. This will also show the company that you are serious about the position. Call the company and ask them for an interview. Here is a sample conversation:

"Good morning. I applied for the _____ position at your company a few days ago. I was calling to follow up and make sure you received it. I would very much like to discuss the position with you further. Is it possible to schedule an appointment?"

By going at it from this angle you are letting the company know that you are serious about the position, that you are not giving up easily, and that you want an interview. You are essentially demanding an interview but in a way that could make them think that it is their idea.

Interview opportunities rarely come to you by themselves. You have to actively ask for an interview or you will never get one. You can use this same tactic when closing your cover letters, such as making the last line "I would like to discuss this position with you further. I look forward to hearing from you." This tells the employer that you are expecting a call.

How to Prepare for an Interview

Preparing for an interview begins before you get the call for an appointment. You should actually start preparing for the interview process when you begin your job search. Much of the preparation for an interview can be used for any interview opportunity to come across.

Your first step in preparing for an interview is to be able to anticipate the questions that the interviewer might ask, and being prepared with an answer. When you formulate these answers ahead of time and rehearse them, you will be able to repeat them easily during an actual interview. This can make you appear more confident, and help the employer see that you are able to meet the challenges of intelligent conversation. It will also take away a lot of the nervousness you feel.

There are countless possible interview questions depending on the industry, field, and position you are interviewing for. Finding sample interview questions specific to your career is easy. You can find many books on the subject, as well as helpful websites and podcasts. A simple Google search will lead you to many resources.

Here are some of the most common interview questions:

Tell me about yourself. (This answer should include where you are in your career, a brief summary about your experience and why you are there, and perhaps some hobbies that relate to the position you are interviewing for.)

Why are you interested in this position? (Make sure you make this about the work itself or the company, not about the benefits or salary.)

Why are you leaving/did you leave your last position? (Give well thought out reasons that are true, but avoid bad mouthing the company, management or coworkers. For example, you can cite the instability of the company, or a lack of advancement opportunities.)

What makes you right for this job? (This is where you can use some of the same things you used in your cover letter, relating your experience and skills to the demands of the position.)

Tell me about a time when…? (Consider any situation that might arise in the position you are interviewing for and formulate answers to those questions using your real experience. This keeps you from having to pause to come up with an answer during the interview.)

What is most important to you in a new position? (Be honest about what you are looking for, but focus on how you can develop your skills and add to your career portfolio. It is also good to say you are looking for a company with advancement opportunities, because this shows a commitment to longevity with the company.)

What salary range are you looking for? (Research what your desired position pays when combined with your level of education and experience so you know what to ask for.)

What questions do you have for me? (While you will want some position and company specific questions to ask, you can formulate some general questions like asking about company culture.)

Preparing for a Specific Interview

Before going into an interview you should be prepared to discuss the specific position and the company. Research as best you can what the position entails and what qualifications would make a good candidate. Make a short list of questions you have about the position. You can ask these questions when the interviewer inevitably asks "What questions do you have for me?"

You should also research the company thoroughly. It is common for an interviewer to ask what you know about the company so far. The more information you can give them the more impressed they will be. By knowing a lot about the company you are showing that you have done your research, know what the company is about, and really want to work for them. It shows how serious you are about winning the position. Researching the company can also give you more ideas for questions to ask at the end of the interview.

Practicing Your Answers

You should practice your answers to likely interview questions in the mirror. You can also video yourself answering them or making an audio recording. After you have finished you can review the recordings and decide how well you did. You can also practice answering interview questions with a partner and get their opinion of how you are doing.

Continue practicing your answers until you feel completely comfortable with them. Remember, you don't know for sure which questions you will be asked or in what order. Your answers must come naturally enough to you that you can answer any question confidently with your pre-formulated answer. The goal here is to prevent yourself from being caught off guard during the interview. It is like learning lines for a play, except you don't know what order they are going to come in. You have to have your cues and your lines memorized together.

Your Appearance

An interviewer's opinion of you can be formulated before you ever say a word. Your appearance will make a huge difference in the success of your interview. In fact, if your interview is very short and not comprehensive, it is likely that the interviewer was put off by your appearance and did not consider you a viable candidate from the moment you walked in the door.

You must consider more than simply what you will wear. Your hair should be neat and styled. It should also be a natural color, even if the employer allows unnatural hair colors with its employees. Avoid fancy hair styles that will make you fidget or wonder if a hair is out of place. It should be comfortable yet professional.

You should also consider your piercings and jewelry. Remove any visible piercings besides earrings. Any bracelets, rings or necklaces should be tasteful and unobtrusive. Your jewelry should not automatically draw the attention of the interviewer. Avoid gaudy or large broaches or pendants. You should also refrain from wearing any type of religious jewelry.

Men should ensure that they are clean shaven, or that their beard and/or mustache are neatly trimmed. It is also considered more professional if side burns do not extend past the top of the ear. Women who wear a skirt or dress should have shaved legs, and women wearing a sleeveless blouse should also shave under their arms. Shaving shows that you have respect for your body and a dedication to cleanliness and good hygiene.

If you have any tattoos you should cover them for the interview, particularly if you are interviewing for a professional or office position. If you have tattoos on your legs, wear slacks. If you have tattoos on your arms, wear long sleeves. If you have tattoos that cannot be covered, such as on your neck or hands, try to downplay them by how you position your body. Hopefully they are not too visible or profound.

Chapter 12: The Interview

Your objective in a meeting is to show your best qualities to the questioner and convince them to hire you for the offered job. The questioner's objective is to assess you on diverse criteria than simply aptitude. There are a few things that you must include in your interview, which are as follows:

Why you need the employment

How you fit the employment capabilities

What you can help the superintendent

Why you need to work for the association

What you have looked into yourself and your work

Besides this, here are a few more tips to help you get you through the main part of the interview process.

Be true, positive, and legit with your replies.

Do not discuss what was off with past employments or past executives.

Relate your experience and achievements to the superintendent's necessities.

Avoid specifying fiscal concerns or individual issues.

Have your resume and/or portfolio with you in an expert looking organizer.

Know The Basis of Assessment

As soon as your interview begins, questioners will deliberately listen and assess your reactions. Notwithstanding your information about the occupation and communication styles, they may search for the accompanying qualities. Some of these qualities are:

What aptitudes do you utilize when connecting with others?

How well do you comprehend the occupation and reach its capabilities?

Can you make fitting inductions and inferences throughout the course of the meeting?

How rationally caution and dependable would you say you are?

Have you utilized great judgment and the ability to think with respect to your life arranging so far?

Do you show a level of erudite profundity when conveying, or is your reasoning shallow and needing profundity?

How well do you react to push and stress?

What is your ability for critical thinking?

Are your replies original or are they copied from any book on interviewing?

In order to address these requirements, you must:

Research the position and association to fit your aptitudes to the occupation.

Present yourself as intrigued and regularly eager about the occupation, not practiced and level.

Some questioners may test you to perceive how you handle stress.

In the event that the meeting is not going easily, don't freeze.

Ask your questioner to rehash anything you don't see so you can accumulate your considerations.

Stay positive.

Interviews May Not Always Be Predictable

At times, inquiries are asked basically to perceive how you respond. So, respond carefully as you are being observed all the time. You must:

Consider the inquiry.

Pause quickly.

Give a characteristic reaction.

Throughout the meeting, you may be asked some abnormal inquiries. You may have to face some shocking questions like "Let me know a joke" to "What has been the best moment of your life?" These are not the sort of inquiries you can plan for ahead of time, yet your response and reaction will be assessed on all these by the interviewer. The key is to remain calm and positive. While these questions may appear weird in the interview scenario, they are questions that can be easily answered of you have calm and composed mind. So, just go for it!

Chapter 13: Groundwork For Interview

You would have read through the pages about the types of questions faced by Roshan along the ups and downs of his career graph. It is likely that you might also get similar type of questions.

This would have given you an insight into how to reply to questions in brief, in detail, without embarrassment and without defaming the self and employer. Whenever you receive a call, you have to do some groundwork before facing the interview. Let's see.

Know about the organisation: Just because your received a call for interview, do not be in a hurry. Browse the internet and know more about its standing reputation, market strength, business review etc. Sometimes websites would appear elite and a personal visit would disprove it.

What is the job role? Do research on job title. The responsibilities of a job title might differ from company to company. It can also be called by any other title. Though an outline of the role and responsibilities for that title remains the same, yet there could be some distinct additions depending on the industry. Look out for the salary survey and see where do you stand and what is the range of salary offered. Compare this at the specialised website by feeding input data like age, job title, educational qualification, location, current drawn salary, benefits and other details.

The graph thus generated shall be for reference purpose only and not as a proof for salary negotiation. Your data that you keyed will also be used for sampling for other searches also. None is sure about the authenticity of data that people like you feed in.

Know the key people on top: You might ask me, 'what am I going to do knowing their names, do I have to tell I know them?' It is only to know more about them in social networking site. You may get to know their educational background and see what you can learn new and how they functioned.

Practice body language: Sit up straight, make eye contact, and shake hands firmly -- in short, practice like someone who deserves to get the job. See that you exhibit all etiquettes and manners termed as (ELQ) Executive-Like-Qualities.

At times it is possible that you may be lacking internal personality. By displaying the good side of your external personality, you can suppress your weak personality but it requires lots of effort. On the other side, if your internal personality is good, you can learn to display yourself externally in a better way. You cannot ask the interviewer to repeat the interview again where you can rectify your mistakes done and start over again. This is not a movie retake. It is a chance that you have to use it at first go. Please recall all the manners exhibited by Roshan. Never try to answer in single word of Yes or No. Add meaning to by expanding your answer in support of it. Never expose egoistic attitude at any time.

Here is a look at the general etiquettes and manners. This will hold good for interviewer, interviewee, and executives in front office, sales, customer care, purchase, banking, counselling, call centre, etc.

• Knocking the door of the cabin of the person you are visiting and taking permission to enter before entering the cabin.

• Always checking up with the executives of the company or their secretaries for an appointment for better time management and show manners.

• Pick up the phone before two to three rings.

• On phone, be polite.

- On phone, answer by giving your company's name, your name and department's name

- Whenever you receive a phone for someone else, take down the name of the caller, his organization name, telephone number and pass them on to the person who was called.

- Never put a caller on the hold for more than a few seconds. In case you wish to do it, take the caller's permission to do so.

- Be punctual for meetings, carry a scribbling pad and pen.

- Always go fully prepared for meetings, keep all the relevant data/information with you.

- Say "good morning", "good evening" according to the time of the day. Shake hands firm and brief seconds. Never keep holding the hand of the person for a long time or shake violently to trigger tremor.

- Do not shake hands with Indian ladies on your own (unless she takes initiative). Say

"Hi" or "namaste" politely with folded hands. Do study the cultural aspects of such greetings and salutations for other cultures too.

• Never say "good night" when you are meeting another person in the evening/night. The correct salutation is "good evening". When you part with him in the night say "good night".

• Try to remember the correct names of the persons with whom you are dealing and address them properly. Never call other person by "hello" or "Sh sh sh" etc. They are bad manners.

• Never keep your mouth open while taking a yawn. Close it by keeping a palm over the mouth. In the first place do not yawn in front of others, control it. It is contagious if once sighted.

• While sitting do not keep shaking your legs or show wide open thighs.

- Keep your mouth clean of bad breath. Do not eat garlic or onions etc during the day time if possible.

- Keep yourself clean and use perfume/deodorant.

- Do not talk/gossip with a fellow colleague sitting next to you during the conduct of meetings or while waiting for interview.

- In case you have to go out of an ongoing meeting, do so without pushing chairs and disturbing others.

- Always offer chair to others for sitting, if you could.

- Do not shout while talking. Always keep your cool.

- You must dress properly, well fitting and clean pressed clothes.

- Do not wear the same socks every day. Wash them and use.

- Polish your shoes regularly.

- Shave daily without any exception (for men).

- Avoid smoking, taking tobacco or pan masala etc in vicinity.

- Never spit along aisle or stairs.

- Cut your nails regularly.

- Comb your hair properly.

- Do not scratch your body or touch private parts in public.

- Rehearse your sentences in mind before you actually speak out.

- Never talk loose.

- Keep diary and make sure that whatever tasks you undertake should be completed in time.

- Never encourage grapevines. You may become a victim.

- Do not have favourites, treat everyone professionally.

- Never leak out company secrets and confidential information. You would have signed an NDA (Non-disclosure agreement).

- If you do not drink, say a polite "no, thanks" for drinks. If you do drink, keep it in limits in parties. Not to vomit in open.

Try to inculcate the above in routine life so that you get used to it.

	From inside	From outside
Good	Strength	Opportunity
Bad	Weakness	Threat

Prepare in advance: By way of your replying by heart to all questions, do not show that you prepared and mugged up. Try to talk extempore. Do not give out answers that were prepared by/for somebody. List out skills based on your SWOT (Strength, Weakness, Opportunities, Threat).

You can only be guided to answer and not to be spoon fed. [By the way, don't learn Roshan's answers by heart and recite in your interview.]

Chapter 14: What Is The Secret To Landing That New Job

Seldom you find an individual who wants to exist but never dreamed of having a good job. He is so irresponsible. He is a selfish person not thinking about his real purpose in this world. You belong to the majority who wants a better job to be able to give the needs of your loved ones. It is good that you are now working but the truth is you are not earning enough to support your family.

The sorrows of not finding a new job

Great disappointment and depression – you were not born to depend on your parents or siblings. You were created to be responsible not just for your loved ones but for yourself as well. A good school and university were given to you to finish your studies which you did. You had high hopes that you would be able to find a good job but the country's economy went down and the company to which you are working for could not give you the salary increase you were asking. Don't lose hope! There are steps you should take to be able to find the right job for you!

Things you should know to help you find that new job

Build your self-confidence – this is a common problem of the graduates. Did you already forget you graduated from a good university with high grades? Don't soak yourself to depression when there is nothing to be depressed of! It was not your fault if you are not earning enough at the present. It was the economy and not you. You have started the first step and that is reading this e-book right now! You don't have reasons to get disappointed. Where is the self-confidence built when you were the student council president? It is not right that you forget one of the good things you developed in the past years. It was built and it will never leave you. It is time to get up and start anew! Re-build your self-confidence to be able to move forward and land the best job for you.

You are a winner – the self-confidence you have makes you a sure winner on your job applications. It is the different companies which will get in touch with you for job offers. How would you like to receive calls from good companies?

Be prepared always – the eagerness you are showing makes job offers comes closer to you. You must be prepared with the things you should do when they come. Be alert on phone calls because it might come at any time of the day. You should be well equipped with knowledge on how you should look in going to your interview. Look and study the tips on how to behave and do well with the interview. All factors should be looked and considered as they all work hand-in-hand to help you get a new and better job.

Stop depression from attacking you because you have a brighter future being accepted to a job fit for your qualifications and realization of your dreams!

Chapter 15: Body Language: Tips For A Confident And Positive Body Language

They say it's not what you say but how you say it.

This is especially true when it comes to job interviews. What comes out of your mouth is just as important as how it comes out of your mouth and the rest of your body.

Although this may sound as a stereotype, most interviewers are HR officers that studied psychology or a related course in college. This means these people have rudimentary knowledge on how to read people's emotions through their body language. There's a good chance they can tell if you're nervous or upset based on how you look during the interview. There's an even bigger chance they can tell if someone really means what they're saying.

This is why your body has to reflect a confident and sincere applicant. Fortunately, this is very easy to attain. If you already have the wardrobe figured out (as explained in the earlier chapter), then your posture and gestures will take care of the rest.

The Handshake

This is one of the most powerful forms of body language you can master. Take note that handshakes mostly happen during first encounters. This means your handshake is part of your first impression; it had better be good.

Go too strong and they might think you're over-assertive and bossy. Go too weak and they might think you're a push-over. Find your middle ground. Try a few handshakes with a friend to see if your grip is too strong or if it needs more effort. Practice is the only way to get this right.

It also not just about your grip and shake. It's also about how you extend your hand. It's better to extend your arm from a bent position than to swing your hand upward from a lowered position. This shows respect. Also make sure to extend your hand with your palms slightly facing downwards. This will show your assertiveness and willingness to take charge of things.

When it comes to the shaking part, try not to take their hands off. A slight jimmy would do as if you were trying open a door with a rusted key. You can also take it a step further by clasping their hand with two hands to show warmth and friendliness. It all depends on the image that you want to project.

Ideally, you want to project an image of confidence with your handshake but not too much so that you come off as arrogant.

Most importantly, you have to be the one initiating the handshake. Do not wait for your interviewer to offer their hands to you; they may not even do that entirely as they could be expecting you to make the first move. This will show how eager you are to be there and to impress them.

Eye Contact

This says a lot more about you than the things you'll actually say. The simple rule here is to look directly at the interviewers' eyes when speaking. It would really look insincere if you were looking away when talking about yourself.

There are also those cases when you find it difficult to look at the interviewer straight. They could have something in their teeth or there's something wrong with their face. In these cases, looking at their forehead is a better alternative.

Sitting

There are a lot of approaches when it comes to how you present yourself in this manner. Depending on the kinds of furniture they have at their office, you will want to keep a few golden rules in mind to make sure you get the best impression.

If they have swivel chairs with cushioned bottoms and backrests, you might end up getting too comfortable and start leaning back. You don't want to do that just yet. Show them that you're sharp and on your toes by sitting at the edge of the seat as you listen to them.

In this position, avoid leaning forward too much, especially if there is only a small space between you and the interviewer. With your back away from the backrest, you'll also avoid leaning back, forcing you to maintain a straight body as you conduct your interview. This is the best position that will show them you're here for serious business.

Then there's also the talk about crossing your legs. Different people will interview this gesture in different ways; so the best thing to do is to avoid crossing them unless the lower part of your body is blocked by a table.

There are people who are more comfortable talking when their legs are crossed; but you have to remember you're there to impress and not get comfortable. Try to avoid crossing your legs as much as possible to avoid hurting your chances by coming off as laid-back.

Although these tips may sound as if you're supposed to be stiff, try not to harden your body and ease yourself into your interview by listening well and responding appropriately.

Hand Gestures

Different people have different ways to explain themselves especially in a business setting. There are those who can handle their points without using hand gestures; then there are also those who are more comfortable using their hands to illustrate their points.

If you're the latter, try keeping your hand gestures within a controllable range. This means that it's alright to use gestures so long as they aren't too distracting and large. Try to keep your elbows bent while you use your hands. This will show them that you're interested in the discussion but aware of the personal space involved as well.

Also, if you plan to point at things in the office to help talk about yourself, try not to use your straightened index finger. Instead use a full opened hand with all fingers pointing somewhere with your palm facing the ceiling.

The Smile (Brush Technique)

Never forget this valuable indicator of confidence. Nothing speaks this better than a person who is happy to be where they are at the moment. Nothing else shows that better than a smile.

Although it is true that different people have different smiles for certain occasions, try to use a simple one that simple shows your gratefulness for the interview.

Try saying the word "brush" for starters. Take note of what you do with your mouth when you do so. You're forced into stretching out those lips to show your teeth. This method is used by professional photographers and models that need good smiles in their pictures.

Try not to overuse it, though. You don't have to be smiling all the time while you're there. That will make you look scripted and unnatural. Simply smile at every joke they make or when you sincerely find something amusing in your conversation.

Overall, never forget to smile when you first meet your interviewer. This is best done when shaking their hand. An enthusiastic and firm handshake coupled with a good smile is the perfect indicator of comfort and confidence that plenty of interviewers hope to find when they engage a potential candidate.

Chapter 16: What To Prepare Before An Interview

Knowing that you have an interview coming up can be stressful. However, if you use the time before your interview to prepare yourself, you will likely look and feel more confident during the interview. This lesson will guide you through different ways to prepare for an interview. It will explain how to research the company beforehand. It will help you identify appropriate interview attire and will provide you with a checklist of items to bring along with you. And it will help you both prepare to ask the right questions and practice answering the questions you are likely to be asked.

Research the company

During an interview, you will need to show an employer that you know about and understand the needs of the company.

One way to prepare for this is to research the company.

In general, you want to find out:

What products or services the company sells.

Who its customers and competitors are.

How the company is doing within the industry.

What the company culture is like.

Other researching tips

Drive to the interview location beforehand—preferably at the same time of day as your interview—so you can get a reasonable estimate of how long the travel time will be on the actual day of your interview. You don't want to be late for an interview!

The actual job description or job posting will likely contain information about the company.

Decide what to wear to an interview

Like most people, interviewers are susceptible to first impressions, and one of the first things an interviewer will see of you is how you're dressed. Because you want to make sure your first impression is a good one, here are some things to keep in mind when choosing an outfit for an interview.

A good interview outfit should be relatively formal, so don't wear jeans, T-shirts, or sneakers unless you've specifically been asked to wear them. A business suit is usually a safe bet for either a man or a woman. If you don't have a business suit, a long-sleeved, solid-colored shirt (button-down for men) or sweater and a pair of dark-colored cotton or wool pants will usually work.

When you choose your clothes, make sure they fit well, are not visibly worn out, and are comfortable to sit down in. Both men and women should avoid wearing clothing that's too tight because provocative clothing isn't seen as professional attire.

Women should avoid low necklines and short skirts for the same reason.

Keep accessories to a minimum. Wearing too much jewelry, makeup, perfume, or cologne is considered unprofessional, and it won't make a good impression on an interviewer. You may even want to avoid perfume or cologne altogether because you have no way of knowing whether any of the people you'll meet are allergic to it.

Wear dark or neutral colors, even if these aren't colors you ordinarily wear. This applies not only to the clothes you wear but also to accessories and shoes. Women should also wear neutral-colored stockings, and men should wear neutral or dark ties.

Make sure you're well-groomed when you're going to an interview. Check that your hair and nails are neat and clean and that your clothing is unwrinkled or ironed before leaving the house. This shows the interviewer that you took the time to prepare for the interview and are taking it seriously.

Keep in mind that not every tip on this list will apply in all situations. For an audition interview, for example, you may be expected to dress less formally, depending on what you'll be asked to do. If you're not sure what to wear, you may be able to call the human resources department of the company and ask what would be appropriate. You can also ask friends or colleagues who may have interviewed at similar workplaces.

Decide what to take with you to an interview

After you've decided what to wear, it's time to think about what you should bring along with you to the interview. It's also important to know what you should leave at home or in your car.

It is best to assemble the items you are bringing along in a briefcase or similar professional-looking organizer. Remember, your first impression should be as a neat, organized, and prepared individual!

Practice answering questions

Because the most significant portion of your interview will be spent answering questions, the best way to prepare for an interview is to anticipate the questions you'll likely be asked and then practice your answers to these questions.

All interviewers will ask some common interview questions to determine if you are the best candidate for the job. These questions usually deal with your career goals, your level of interest in the job and company, your job skills and motivation, and your interpersonal communication skills.

Prepare your questions to ask

An interview is as much for you as it is for the hiring manager. It is your chance to find out more about the job, the company, the industry, and your potential boss. Your questions should show your genuine interest in or understanding of the company. Knowing which questions to ask and which not to ask can help you get more out of your interview—and can perhaps even get you the job!

If you don't ask any questions during your job interview, the hiring manager may believe you're not interested in the job! On the other hand, asking specific questions might give the hiring manager the same impression. Avoid questions about salary or benefits until you've been offered the job.

Chapter 17: Your Focus

Pay attention to yourself on purpose,

in the present moment, without judgment.

Who You Are

UP TO THIS POINT, you've explored the impact of fear and anxiety on the human brain, and you've discovered strategies you can employ to inspire your creativity and overcome habitual thought patterns and limitations.

From this point forward, the path you're on leads into a clearing.

Here, your focus is on remembering your strengths and affirming the reality of who you really are.

All of the parts of you; your experiences; your family history; your gender and birth order; the exposure you've had to art, culture, and education; the people you've encountered; your health and physical abilities; moments spent in nature; your connection to beloved pets, and wild things; instances of joy, and anguish, and heartbreak; the creative sparks that shaped you; challenges and risks that emboldened you; your place in time; stretches of playfulness; your memories; the learning journey you've embraced – every bit of the being that is you – all of this and more, together, has wrought the whole of you, and carved into the deepest parts of you your inner strengths, personal attributes, skills, accomplishments, achievements, interests, and your future hopes and dreams.

You are a singular, remarkable human. There's no one like you. It's time for you to remember all of who you are, and for you to begin to think about the transferable nature of your strengths and qualities, and the enormous value that you contribute in your life, and that you bring to the world of work.

It's easy to get stuck here, in this place of strength, clarity, and illumination, mostly because the memories of being hurt, which are stored in the emotional brain, might feel they are under attack by your awakening strengths inside that have long been in the shadows.

Notice the ways you try to avoid moving forward through this chapter!

You'll need to rely heavily on your willingness to over-ride distractions – all forms of physical discomfort, including hunger, moments of annoyance, and especially feelings of fatigue. Notice your reactions, smile (I am a nerd), and record your insights in your notebook.

There's extraordinary value for you to journal about the thoughts that are activated during these focussed exercises.

Stay in, and dig deep.

Exchange habit for habit as you overcome your automatic thoughts, and begin now to predict your future success.

Write, record, jot down, and journal your thoughts. Then write some more.

Choose words and phrases that demonstrate how you're a fit for the job for which you want to apply.

Formulate a personal example of how and when you've demonstrated each strength, skill, and personal attribute. During interviews you'll be asked in countless different ways to give examples of your strengths and skills. That's not the best time for you to test your memory and sort through past experiences.

You'll send a powerful message when you match your strengths, skills, and attributes to the needs of the job for which you're applying. This is easy to accomplish –

first think of the requirements of the job, and then reflect on instances when you've embodied those particular traits.

Again, jot all of it down!

Strengths and Personal Attributes

I AM (choose and write down your personal attributes – who you are)

Choose at least 3 from the columns below, or substitute with personal attributes that are not listed.

Punctual	Responsible	Self-motivated
Tidy	Detail-oriented	Willing to learn
Curious	Persistent	People-oriented
Organized	Trustworthy	Efficient
Attentive	Cooperative	Eager
Patient	Friendly	Persuasive
Enthusiastic	Quick learner	Willing
Careful	Positive and helpful	Good listener
Health	Dependable	Flexible

conscious

Loyal	Respectful	Good communicator
Considerate	Confident	Adaptable
Creative	Tolerant	Resilient
Appropriate	Truthful	Tenacious
Forthright	Capable	Energetic
Discerning	Courageous	Cool under pressure
Kind	Analytic	Self-starter
Sincere	Collaborative	Precise

A STRENGTH I HAVE: I AM …

A STRENGTH I HAVE: I AM …

A STRENGTH I HAVE: I AM …

Skills

I HAVE THE FOLLOWING SKILLS

(write about what you have experience doing)

Choose 2 or 3 skills from the columns below, or substitute with skills that are not listed:

Teamwork	Communicator	Cashiering
Sales experience	Technical aptitude	Computer experience
Problem-solving	Documentation	Hosting
Word processing	Decision-making	Social media
Cooking and Prep	Time management	Leadership

Customer service	Shipping	Receiving
Hands-on	Work under pressure	Serving
Self-managing	Relationship building	Researching
Trouble-shooting	Sorting	Multi-tasking
Bussing tables	French speaking	Goal-setting
Critical thinking	Greeting customers	Filing
Automotive repair	Attention to detail	Cataloguing

I AM SKILLED AT:

I AM SKILLED AT:

I AM SKILLED AT:

Accomplishments and Achievements

Search through your memories and write about your achievements with pride.

Use this list to prompt yourself and/or nudge your memory and make note of several of your accomplishments.

I AM PROUD THAT I:

Have a Bronze Cross in swimming.

Delivered newspapers 3 times a week for 2 years.

Taught myself to play guitar.

Graduated high school.

Earned a black belt in Tae Kwon Do.

Quit smoking

Babysit for neighbours and family.

Cut and weed grandparents' lawn.

Sang alone on stage.

Volunteered at summer camp.

Helped my father build a shed.

Earned my airfare for a family trip

Passed the exam for First Aid Level 2.

Competed internationally on a ski team.

Routinely cook dinner once a week for my siblings.

Returned to high school and graduated.

Left home at 15 and support myself.

Lost 20 lbs. since last summer

Play piano by ear.

Tutor my sister who has an anxiety disorder.

Work out and eat well.

Have my driver's license.

I AM PROUD THAT I:

I AM PROUD THAT I:

I AM PROUD THAT I:

Interests

List the activities you enjoy or that you have a desire to try some day:

Choose 2 or 3. Explain how or why the activity interests you, or substitute with activities that are not on this list.

I AM INTERESTED IN

Acting	Animal rescue	Baking
Building	Construction	Climbing
Cooking	Collecting	Drawing
Fixing things	Cycling	Fishing
Playing guitar	Popular culture	Skiing
Listening to music	Learning new things	Sewing
Playing hockey	Watching movies	Martial arts

Renovating	Playing soccer	Researching
Snowboarding	Reading mysteries	Swimming
Riding long board	Social media	Travelling
Mountain biking	Studying languages	Video gaming
Working out	Singing	Painting and crafts

I HAVE AN INTEREST IN:

I HAVE AN INTEREST IN:

I HAVE AN INTEREST IN:

Future Hopes and Dreams

Use action words whenever you talk about your future hopes and dreams.

Choose 2 or 3 from this list, or substitute with some of your hopes and dreams that are not listed:

IN THE FUTURE I WANT TO:

Drive a forklift	Succeed at college
Attend cooking school	Learn to drive a car
Become a firefighter	Learn a language
Cheer at the Super Bowl	Play guitar
Sky dive	Buy a car
Hitchhike through Europe	Graduate high school
Start a business	Travel to Asia
Speak in public	Enter an apprenticeship
Buy a condo	Serve the public
Progress in my job	Start a family

Join the police department	Design kitchens
Repair cars	Grow within a career
Learn to cashier	Train to be a florist
Be a builder/contractor	Compete in a triathlon

ONE OF MY DREAMS IS:

ONE OF MY DREAMS IS:

ONE OF MY DREAMS IS:

This chapter, Chapter 17 – Your Focus, has taken you on a journey through your past, your present, and your imagined future.

Whether you've found suitable examples from the lists provided, or you've opted for other words and phrases to describe your strengths, skills, accomplishments, achievements, interests, and your future hopes and dreams, the insight you've assembled with this inventory is substantial.

The best way to show what you can do, is to show what you can do.

Chapter 18: Crafting Your Cover Letter

Now that you understand what a cover letter is and its importance, it is time to learn how to craft your own well-written letter, also known as a CV.

While there are many dos and don'ts in writing a cover letter, thankfully, there is a basic pattern that every professional cover letter should follow.

You can use this guideline with your own information to ensure that your CV is always the correct format.

A basic no-fuss cover letter should consist of:

- Your Name
- Phone number
- Email address
- Date

- Addressed to the name and professional title of the hiring manager

- Name of the company you are applying for a position at

This is the most basic of cover letter guidelines, as you can see, it doesn't even contain much information on the individual. This is because while the standard guideline above is needed, the rest of the letter can be highly personalized.

Along with the above guideline, you also must add other information. This can include a variety of components, depending upon the person. Some options include:

- The address of your professional website

- Your professional title

- Your home address

- Links to your LinkedIn or Twitter

- City of Residence

While you want to illustrate your personality in your cover letter, it is important to do so in a professional manner.

For instance, you want to use an email address that illustrates professionalism. Such as [your name]@gmail.com or email@[your website].com.

You never want to include unprofessional email addresses on your cover letter or resume, as this can be a deal breaker. If your email is something such as SexyTiger135@gmail.com or CottonCandyFTW@yahoo.com you will want to create a new email address for professional purposes.

Ideally, you want to stick with either Gmail or an email created with your own website domain, as these are seen as the most professional options.

Similarly, you should avoid using an email address that contains your current work information.

If your professional email address contains your current company or position, it is disrespectful to both your previous company and the new company to use this address.

Lastly, ensure that your contact information is consistent across the board. You want your resume, cover letter, and social media to all use the same information.

You now understand the basic format of your cover letter and the most important information to include in each and every CV. However, these are only the bare bones of a cover letter.

You still need to include information that will make the employer want to hire you. For that, follow the tips below to get a customized and successful letter.

Use the Proper Format

The cover letter, while it can show your personality, needs to remain professional.

For this reason, use the same formal format that you would for any professional or business matter.

For this, you want to use either Times New Roman, Calibri, or Arial fonts in size twelve or ten point.

When writing your name, contact information, and date align them along the top of the letter. Lastly, keep the cover letter to a single page with three or four short paragraphs.

Address the Hiring Manager

Some people may address this cover letter's to "whom it may concern," but this is bad practice.

This will make it appear that you either have not done enough research on the company or that you are mass producing this CV to send out to multiple companies.

Instead, you want to directly address your letter to the person who will be hiring you. This person's name may be written in the job posting.

However, if it is not, then try calling the main phone number for the company and asking for both the name and position of the hiring manager.

This may seem like an unnecessary step; however, it will leave a big impression on the hiring manager and increase your likelihood of getting hired.

This will also give you the opportunity to learn more about the company in general.

If you have any personal connections to the company and would-be colleges then feel free to subtly mention these connections.

By doing this, it gives the hiring manager the opportunity to ask the people who know you their opinion of your work ethic and capability.

Use Keywords

Often times, employers don't simply read through every cover letter they receive. Instead, they may run it through a filtering software that is meant to scan for keywords in resumes.

This software allows an employer to wade through resumes and cover letters, only reading those that match their preferred keywords of desired skills and experience.

In order to get your cover letter read, you need to naturally and conversationally incorporate key phrases and words that fit the job's description.

You can do this by mentioning how many years of experience you have, degree type, developed skills, communication and organization abilities, and any history you have in project management.

Some examples of keywords to use include:

- Skill Keywords:

- Planned, wrote, analyzed, designed, quantified, programmed, trained, taught, surveyed, organized, critiqued, inspected, assembled, solved, engineered, maintained, operated, administered, appraised, audited, budgeted, calculated, projected, researched, directed, developed, performed, acted, established, fashioned, illustrated, founded, programmed, coached, communicated, instructed, enabled, encouraged, guided, informed, built.

- Result-Oriented Keywords:

- Implemented, planned, managed, upgraded, assessed, strengthened, persuaded, initiated, adapted, oversaw, lead, redesigned, helped, launched, began, adopted, boosted, headed, operated, increased, trained, educated, reformulated, expanded, acquired, generated, produced, initiated.

- Self-Descriptive Keywords:

- Independent, creative, unique, attentive, dependable, responsible, ambitious, analytical, sensitive, reliable, enthusiastic, adaptable, logical, initiative, efficient, experienced, effective, sincere, productive, personable, instrumental, honest, adept, loyal, diplomatic, insightful.

Keep the First Paragraph Strong

At the beginning of your letter, you should start with a strong and personal greeting directly to the hiring manager.

But, don't slack off after this greeting.

It is vital to have a strong opening paragraph that catches their attention and draws them into reading your entire letter and your resume.

This means that you absolutely must avoid any misspellings or typos.

You also need to include something interesting about yourself that sets you apart from the crowd.

While the entire cover letter is important, the most important areas to strengthen are the beginning and then end.

After all, it is vital to make a good first impression and leave off with a good impression.

Highlight Relevant Details

In your cover letter, you are able to go into more detail on how and why you are a perfect fit for a job.

While a resume simply highlights your experience, the cover letter explains why this experience makes you an ideal fit.

Therefore, when highlighting your experiences, be sure to stick with experiences and reasoning that fits the specific job.

For instance, if you were a waiter and are now applying to a job in another field, it may not at first appear that it is a relevant experience. Yet, the cover letter allows you to explain why this experience actually makes you the best fit. You can take the time to explain that your interactions with customers, managing disputes, and working as a team will enable you to better do the new job, if you are hired. If possible, try to use data and numbers to explain your strengths, as employers like to see hard numbers.

Tie Yourself to the Company

Whenever possible, speak of yourself in relation to the company.

This will show the hiring manager that you have knowledge of the company and convey enthusiasm.

You can do this by mentioning how much you care about the company's vision or mission.

If you have followed the company or used their products/services of years, you can mention how much they have beneficially impacted your life.

Similarly, you want to speak within the letter as if you have already been hired.

For instance, imagine that you are speaking to a manager after being hired and they ask why you chose the company.

You can answer with your interest in the company and enthusiasm about working for them.

For instance: "When I discovered DreamCloud Animation was hiring, I simply knew I must apply. I had been searching for a company that truly makes a difference, where I could make an impact. I was inspired by the company and their mission to consistently produce high-quality animation that tells a story to warm people hearts and increase the appreciation of the seemingly mundane. I believe in the mission of DreamCloud Animation, and I wanted to work with you so that I too can make a difference."

Name the Position Title

It may seem simple, but it is important to add in the name of the job title you are applying for.

This helps the employer to know that you are knowledgeable and understand what you are applying for.

This can be done easily, as you can say something to the effect of "Regarding the Graphic Design position," or "I am writing to apply for Floor Manager position [company name] recently advertised."

Illustrate How You Can Solve a Specific Problem

Are you a problem-solver? While stating this in a cover letter may seem beneficial, it actually has little impact on the hiring manager.

After all, what problems can you solve? By simply stating you are a problem-solver you might as well be saying you know how to "solve" the problem of not knowing what to eat for breakfast when the pantry is nearly bare.

Instead of telling the hiring manager that you are great at solving problems, detail exactly what problems you can help them solve.

How can you use your skills to help the company better and solve their problems? Take time to consider exactly what you can do for the company and then detail it.

Share a Story

You want your cover letter to be captivating, interesting, and informative.

One of the most successful ways in which you can do this is by sharing a story or anecdote about yourself.

This can allow the employer to get a better idea of your personality, work style, and skills. Although, it is important to share the right story while keeping it short and sweet.

How do you know if a story is right for your cover letter?

You can start by looking at the job description and researching the company.

Once you understand the position and company well, you can compare your skills, talents, and experience compared to what they are looking for in an employee.

For instance, the company might be looking for a team player, someone with communication skills, and a person who is able to resolve conflicts, and a person who is able to train those under them.

Keeping these aspects in mind, you can consider your past and think of an anecdote that contains as many of these traits as possible.

For instance, you might have volunteered at a place in which you managed a team, kept everyone on good terms while resolving conflicts, trained newcomers, and communicated the needs of the day to those working with you.

You can share this anecdote, while specifically mentioning these skills and traits you made use of.

By being able to hear a story of how you specifically have used your skills and traits in the past a company can get a better idea of how you will work on the job.

Stay Honest

The worst mistake you can make in your cover letter is being dishonest.

Not only does this have moral implications, but it will also come back to bite you.

If you tell the company that you have an experience, talent, or skill that you don't actually have, then they will find out in the future.

They will soon learn that you are unable to do what you stated, and it will get you into trouble.

Instead, stay honest while putting your best foot forward and highlighting your actual skills and traits in the most positive light possible.

Be You, Stay Unique

The cover letter is created to set you apart from the crowd, which your resume alone is unable to do.

Yet, many people fail to capture any of their unique qualities into their CV, leaving the hiring manager unimpressed and on their way to the next candidate.

This all too often happens when a person uses phrases such as "Hello, I am John/Jane Smith. I am a hard-working, multi-tasking, and detail-oriented person. I was born to be a leader and believe I could help your company."

A hiring manager or employer isn't going to be interested in a basic cover letter template that sounds as if it could be created by anyone. Highlight how you are unique and stand out from the crowd.

You can do this by switching out common words. For instance, instead of saying you are a "natural-born leader" you might say "I excel when leading a team."

This helps your cover letter to sound different, catching a person's eye better.

However, the best way you can stay unique is to share your stories and personality.

Work these into the letter by sharing with the hiring manager stories and examples of how you can best help the company, excel in the position, and make use of your strengths.

Illustrate Your Goals, Passions, and Dreams

An employer doesn't only want to know your strengths and why you are qualified for a position, they also want to know why you care and the career path you envision.

After all, they know that the more passionate a person is about their work the more motivated they are to do a job well done.

If you are passionate about the career, express this. If you dream about becoming a manager and leading a team, let them know.

If your goal is to advance in your field, don't hesitate to add that.

An example: "Graphic design and integrating it into advertisements has been my passion for many years, which is why I pursued my degree in graphic design at New York University. Not only do I dream of working in this field, but I believe my skills will help me to excel. My enthusiasm, passion, and work ethic will push me forward to new heights, making me a wonderful candidate for the position of Graphic Designer at Think! Advertisements."

End on a High Note

When concluding your cover letter in the last paragraph, be sure to use one or two sentences to reiterate why you are the perfect candidate for the job.

As most people will read the resume directly after the cover letter, you want to use this final paragraph to highlight anything important that you want the manager to notice following in your resume.

After you have reiterated anything important, you want to mention that you have attached your resume and that you are looking forward to hearing back from them.

You might even give them a date by which you will contact them if you don't hear back.

For instance: "Thank you for taking the time to consider me for the position of Graphic Designer. I hope my resume, which I have included, proves to be helpful. I look forward to hearing back from you in the near future. I will stay in touch, making a phone call in one week, unless I hear back from you in the meantime."

Unique Visual Format

Humans naturally remember something when it stands out from the crowd. For this reason, instead of simply typing out and printing your cover letter, it is a good idea to give it a unique visual format.

However, this must be done carefully. You don't want to use bright and flashy gimmicks that will turn off the reader or make it more difficult to focus on the contents of the letter. This means that you want to avoid brightly colored paper, unusual fonts, more than two types of fonts, or colored fonts for the letter contents.

The cover letter must remain professional and easy to read.

If you do choose to play around with the visual format, look at some of our examples below to get an idea of what works.

While you want the body text of the letter to use black ink, you might decide to use a dark blue or green ink for the heading text.

Adding a picture of yourself doesn't hurt, as long as it doesn't take up too much of the page space.

Try to arrange your text on the page so that it is visually appealing, rather than appearing in one big difficult to read block.

While you shouldn't use brightly colored paper, you can use a high-quality white or off-white paper.

Conclusion

Starting a new job can be exciting and nerve wracking. Meeting new people, going to new places, and starting out with a blank slate, are all things which can make you feel insecure and uncertain. Remember that the choice to begin a new position is a choice which was made to help you take steps forward in your career. The fact that you have gained a new position over hundreds of other applicants is a testament not only to your interview skills but you as a person. You were the best fit for the position!

Take time out to enjoy the transition phase of starting a new job or career. Pat yourself on the back and be grateful at the opportunity before you. There are many people who wanted the job you have and were not offered a position. Now is the time to focus on showing your company they made the right choice in choosing you as their star candidate.

Do not be surprised if the position you take shifts and changes over time. It can very well be that as the company gets to know your skills better, they may shift your duties slightly to give you the best chance at success. Be sure to communicate openly with your supervisors, while you continue your work efforts, to be certain you are remaining on the same thought path for your career and involvement in the company.

If you find yourself becoming interested in other aspects of the company do not be afraid to vocalize this fact. The more in tune you are with your goals and desires, and the more you communicate with your superiors, the easier it will be to transition into other positions if the opportunity arises. There is nothing wrong with realizing you desire a completely different career path down the line than what you have accepted. It is best to try and remain in a position, unless given a promotion or are moved by the company itself, for at least three years.

The reason for this is because every company likes to see longevity and commitment to the positions you have already taken. People who move from one position to another quickly are also more likely to jump ship. You do not want your new employer to lose faith in your loyalty and excitement for the position you have taken.

Continue to practice your interview skills even if you are happy within your current position. Take time to practice with friends, even acting as the interviewer, and keep your resume up to date. When you have been in a position for a while it can become way to easy to become complacent and lose touch with what an interview is like. Should you desire to apply for a position higher up within the company you may attempt to rely solely on your work merits. Doing this may keep you from being the shining star you were when you gained the position which started you in the company to begin with. Even though you have started the position of your dreams it is always helpful to remain on your game.

Even if you are happy to remain in your position for the rest of your life be sure to take time for yourself and stay excited about your job and the company. Take your vacation time when you can and allow yourself rest and relaxation. Working too much is an easy trap to fall into as people with flourishing careers often feel they are unable to take time off as they are too pivotal to the company function.

If you are constantly working and never taking time for your private life you will easily burn out and begin to hate the job you originally loved. Keeping the passion alive may require effort but it will not require as much effort as trying to rekindle the relationship you once had should it start to fizzle. Set clear boundaries with your work place when you take your position so you are clear about the expectations of the hours you are required to work. If possible take time to reaffirm these boundaries if they are being crossed over time because it will be a necessary practice to keep your heart in your work.

Remind yourself over time what aspects of your job you love. Keep positive affirmations at the ready to continue providing a positive attitude for yourself. There will be bad days at your job as every job has difficulties. No place of employment is perfect but you can be extremely happy if you have taken the time to apply for positions which truly fit who you are.

Your job does not define who you are but it is a big aspect of the building blocks that make you. Being in a positions which you find fulfilling and rewarding will help you in your career path forward and keep you in a positive and happy mindset in the workplace. That positivity will then transfer over to your colleagues and will create an all around better atmosphere.

Be grateful for the new opportunity and rejoice in the fact that you have taken another step closer to your achieved dreams and goals. Your hard work has finally paid off and will continue to do so as you keep bringing all of the wonderful talents you poses to the table. Congratulations on your new position and look forward to the future you will manifest for yourself.

www.ingramcontent.com/pod-product-compliance
Lightning Source LLC
Chambersburg PA
CBHW072013070526
44583CB00015B/1464